THE LEVELED UP LIFE

DAVID ATKINS

THE LEVELED UP LIFE

THE NO EXCUSE BLUEPRINT TO LIVE A LIFE UP TO YOUR FULLEST POTENTIAL

ISBN 979-8-9862869-2-1 (Paperback)
ISBN 979-8-9862869-1-4 (e-Book)
ISBN 979-8-9862869-2-1 (audio Book)

First Printing

Editor: Catherine Leek of Green Onion Publishing
Cover and Interior Design and Layout: Kim Monteforte of Kim Monteforte Book Design & Self-Publishing Services

This book is dedicated to my best friend,
Trooper David C. Brinkerhoff, who was
killed in the line of duty on April 25, 2007.
Our friendship can never be replaced and
what I learned from him and the impact he
made on my life will never be forgotten.

Thank you Brink for watching over
me and my family each day.

CONTENTS

As I sit here at my desk, I am filled with gratitude to live a life on my terms, a life I like to call the Leveled Up Life. I'm happily married, a dad of three daughters, a retired New York State Police Captain of twenty-two years, a million-dollar business earner, and a keynote motivational speaker.

I am my own boss. I live life on my terms. I have freedom and flexibility that I never thought were possible. But how did this happen?

I'm only forty-four years old; this shouldn't be the norm. People often look at me cross-eyed when I tell them I retired at my age. Shouldn't I still be working a nine-to-five job like the vast majority of people late into my sixties or seventies? Isn't that when you retire? How did I end up here? Maybe I should call it "realigned."

I am a regular guy who grew up on Long Island; a son of a police officer and retail executive who lived an everyday life. My parents divorced when I was fourteen, but so did many other parents. I'm nothing special. I didn't come from wealth or ever have anything handed to me in my life. So, when I ask myself how this happened, a few things come to mind – some principles if you will.

Since I was a little boy, I always had a vision and always wanted to be the best I could be at everything. Giving up, not giving 100 percent, or purely quitting was never an option. I failed at many things, but I never stopped until success was met.

This attitude continues through to today. My work ethic, the vision I have, the life lessons I learned, and so much more molded me into the person I am today. Getting here wasn't an overnight success but rather a journey of choices and decisions I made along the way.

It was never about what happened to me that made the difference. It was how I reacted to what happened to me. It was my attitude in choosing to respond positively. Whether it was my parents' divorce, the loss of someone close to me, the challenges I faced with the State Police, or building a business, it all came down to one thing – I never gave up, and I always gave it my best. That is how I ended up here today and why I call this book *The Leveled Up Life*.

I was willing to do things that most weren't willing to do. There was nothing fancy but simple life lessons I consistently applied along my life journey. But now I want to share them with you. I want to share with you these extraordinary lessons that propelled me to where I am today. Some of them overlap and you may read about them more than once because they are that important to your growth. I feel deep in my heart that even applying a few of these principles can drastically change your life and sometimes you need to hear certain points more than once – not just so you can live the Leveled Up Life but because you deserve to live it. It's time to stop playing small, just

> THE WEALTHIEST PLACE ON EARTH IS THE GRAVEYARD. IT IS FULL OF GOALS, IDEAS, AND DREAMS NEVER ACTED UPON.

flowing through life each day. It's time to take control to live your best life.

Before you start, here is my best tip for you as you read this book. *Don't* just soak it all in and feel inspired and motivated. That does nothing for you in the end. The wealthiest place on earth is the graveyard. It is full of goals, ideas, and dreams never acted upon. Don't become part of that stat. Instead, I want to empower you to take what you've learned and immediately apply it to *your* life. If something resonates with you, underline it. Put a yellow sticky note on the page so you can quickly come back to it. Read this book twice. Sometimes it's not about reading ten different books, but reading the same book ten times. That's what I often do. I take a lot more away each time I read the same book. A book speaks to us differently as we travel through different stages of our lives.

Through all my years of growth and success, my best teachers and mentors have come from the books that I read. I say this because I know so often, when you are just starting on the journey to elevate your life, the right people to help you usually are not in the circle of people you are with each day. That's why there are books like this, books that are available to anyone so you, too, can learn what it takes to get there.

Remember that God's gift to us is potential. Our gift back is what we do with it. Live your life with excellence. Absorb what I share and take action so you can live *The Leveled Up Life*, aka your best life. I want the best for you and your family. But in the end, I can only meet you half-way. What you do with what I give you will make the difference. That's the other half – and that's on you.

I close this introduction with this thought. I believe in you. If no one else believes in you, remember that I do. You can achieve anything you put your mind to. As a regular guy, if I can do it, so can you. Let's do this. It's time to get to work!

PART ONE

THE PRINCIPLES
REVEALED

CHAPTER 1

CASTING VISION

"Vision is the art of seeing what is invisible to others."
Jonathan Swift

I loved the game of baseball growing up. Being outside, the nice weather, the smell of new leather coming from your glove, being with friends, the crack of the bat when the ball was hit, and the feel of a brand-new, white baseball. It was heaven.

At twelve years old, I had goals and dreams of being a Major League Baseball player – pretty much like every other boy out there who played baseball. Everything revolved around the game. I would sit in school all day and think about practice or my game that night. I would watch my New York Mets on television, always envious of being a Major League Baseball player one day. (Yes, I am a Mets fan from New York, and it hasn't been easy.) Baseball was life.

In the off-season I couldn't wait for baseball to start. It would always kick off with the baseball parade. I remember feeling like a pro player in that parade, wearing my new uniform with my crisp white pants. It was magical.

I knew at twelve years old that I wanted to improve my game as much as possible and be the best I could be. One day after travel team practice, I remember going to my friend's house to hang out and practice some more. He was a teammate of mine and was one of the best players on our team, a true gem. His older brother was also a baseball star and was drafted by the Detroit Tigers in 1996. The whole family was very athletic.

When I got to his house and walked into his backyard, I couldn't believe what I saw. A full-size batting cage. Yes, a batting cage! In his backyard! Say what? Imagine having that in your backyard. It was a long net with a pitching machine inside. The pitching machine had three light blue legs and two white tires spinning on the top. I'll never forget what it looked like. To get in the batting cage, you simply lifted the net off the ground, stepped inside by home plate, and got into your batting stance as the machine fired out the balls. I was blown away! But something else happened that day. A vision of mine was born.

I, too, wanted a batting cage in my backyard! I literally could picture it in my backyard. I knew exactly where it would go and envisioned all my teammates coming over to hang out and practice. I was excited just thinking about it. Could this be the answer to fulfilling my childhood dreams of going pro? Get a batting cage so I can practice all day to be the very best? Was this the answer? At twelve years old, I sure felt like it was, but the bigger question was how I would do this. How am I going to get this? Simple. Let me ask Mom and Dad.

I remember approaching my mom nervously in the kitchen, preparing to ask her if they would be willing to buy me a batting cage like my friend. I hesitantly asked in a low voice, "Mom, could you and Dad get me a batting cage like my friend Angelo has?" I was unsure how she would respond, but I think I already knew.

My mom replied, "David, a batting cage is *very* expensive, so if you want to get this, you will have to save up for it yourself."

Inside I was saying to myself, "Umm me? Say what? How?" I knew the total cost was $3000! The pitching machine was one outlay, and the netting was another, so it was about $3000. Now, remember I'm twelve, and it's 1989! That is a ton of money back then. Heck, that is a good amount of money even today! How was I going to make this happen?

I couldn't stop thinking about the "how." How was I going to save up for this? I wasn't sure how, but I knew one thing for certain. I was going to do whatever it took to make this happen. I believed this so strongly that I wrote my parents a note, a very powerful one as I look back today. My mom kept this note, and I have the privilege of sharing it with you today. It's stained and tattered, sitting under an angel paperweight, partially in the frame on top. But it is a clear reminder of the vision I had and how serious I was.

It reads, "I, David Atkins, say I can save up for a pitching machine. I believe in myself. Signed, David Atkins."

> LITTLE DID I KNOW BACK THEN ABOUT THE POWER OF WRITING SOMETHING DOWN AND HOW I WAS CASTING A VISION FOR SOMETHING I WANTED TO ACCOMPLISH.

Little did I know back then about the power of writing something down and how I was casting a vision for something I wanted to accomplish. I'm sure my mom thought it was cute, but I was as serious as a twelve-year-old could be, if that meant anything. Just merely thinking about the goal and dream wasn't enough. I had to put pen to paper, share it with my parents, and cast the vision for myself that I would look at every single day. In an unexpected way, I held myself accountable for reaching that goal. I knew it would be challenging, but I also knew it wouldn't be impossible.

I found a local newspaper delivery route for the Long Island newspaper, *Newsday*, that I quickly learned could become my potential answer. I inquired more about it, and *Newsday* sent a gentleman to my house to talk to me about it. I immediately accepted the job when it was offered to me.

It was for the daily newspaper delivery to about thirty houses in the area. It was seven days a week. On Mondays through Fridays I would deliver the paper right after school. On Saturday, I would deliver the paper mid-morning, but it was a different animal on Sunday. Why? Everyone wanted their Sunday paper early, and it was also a much thicker newspaper. It meant getting up super early (usually by six o'clock in the morning) and taking extra time to put the different sections of the paper together.

The papers were usually dropped at the bottom of our driveway each day for delivery. But all those different sections for Sunday's paper came a day early, on Saturday. The Sunday paper delivery started the night before by putting all the sections together. It was tedious and took a while. I would lay out all the sections on the floor in our family room, often with the television on so I could watch a baseball game while putting them together. Then on Sunday morning, when the news section was delivered, I added that main section, and off I went on deliveries.

I used my favorite blue BMX Mongoose bike to deliver the newspapers. There was no place to hold the newspapers, so I would take a piece of worn, yellow rope from our garage and tie it around an old milk crate and onto the front handlebars. I added a basket to the front of my bike. It wasn't that secure, so it would constantly bounce around while I rode my bike. The daily fun I had jumping over curbs at the edge of driveways didn't happen while delivering the newspapers, or else I would have ended up with two black eyes.

This went on for seven days a week for well over a year. It would rain on me. Snow on me. Sleet on me. I had to deal with every season of weather living in New York, which meant frigid winters and sweltering summers. There were more days than I could count that I didn't want to do the work. I was cold. I was tired from school. I was sweating from the heat. It was grueling work, especially in the bad weather for a twelve-year-old.

The worst part was collecting, that is, collecting the money from customers to pay for the newspaper. Smartphones, Venmo, Zelle, etc., didn't exist. To get paid, I had to go to every person's house, knock on their door, and hope they were home to pay me. I used an index card to keep track of everyone. I would write down everyone's name, creating a list with many columns to track the payment for each week. A simple "x" in a column meant they paid.

It wasn't easy to collect. Often no one answered. Many who did, told me to come back because they didn't have the money. Sometimes people would even be behind a few weeks. It was always an uphill battle. What made it more challenging was that I relied on tips to make most of my money. Some would barely tip me; a few would tip well. A good tip was over $1 in 1989. It cost about $3.50 a week, so I was super excited if I got $5. This was a big deal. But in the end, I had to follow up with people a lot which was much work.

This went on for over a year, but after being consistent, never giving up, maintaining the discipline to do it even when I didn't feel like it, along with a few other persevering actions, I eventually hit my benchmark! I saved that $3000! I remember walking up to my parents and telling them I had saved the money, but more importantly, proving I could do it. I honestly didn't know if they believed me at first.

I then followed through and bought the same batting cage and pitching machine as my friend. My dad helped by building the frame using two-by-fours, so I didn't need to add that expense. My dream of having a batting cage in my backyard at twelve years old became a reality. It was epic!

I remember school buses and cars stopping in front of our house to see what it was because it was situated on the left side of our house. It was big and hard to miss looking from the road. Some even thought it was a bird sanctuary! But nope. It was a baseball batting cage bought by a twelve-year-old boy with a vision.

What I truly learned at the age of twelve was worth more than $3000. It is something that any of us can apply to our life today. It's something I continue to do every day as I strive for new goals. Anytime you want to achieve something, you have to cast a vision for it. It has to be so powerful that you literally can close your eyes and see it. You must feel it. You must see it. You must taste it. You must write it down as I did. It has to be so powerful that it feels as if it's already here.

You can't wait for your mom, dad, brother, sister, or spouse to

> **ANYTIME YOU WANT TO ACHIEVE SOMETHING, YOU HAVE TO CAST A VISION FOR IT.**

support you. If you want something, you need to go out there and get it! It is no one else's job to support your goals and dreams but you. Sometimes you will need to be your own hero to make this happen. It will be lonely. You may feel isolated at times on this journey by yourself. But it will be worth it! After achieving something you cast a vision for, the sense of accomplishment and subsequent hard work is priceless. It's something money can't buy.

You need to write it down and have it in a place where you can see and read it every day. Your mind is a powerful tool. When you read something every day, it has an interesting way of aligning your subconscious mind, so your thoughts and feelings become more creative and support achieving that goal. Hang it on your bathroom mirror. Put it on your fridge. It doesn't matter where you put it, but write it down and find a place where you will see it each day.

On the left side of my desk, leaning on my iMac screen is a big index card with my keynote speaking goals for the following year. In my bedroom, I also have a vision board. It's nothing fancy. It's a bulletin board hung on the wall like a picture frame. There are pictures of other things I want to accomplish. For example, a vacation home, a new deck with a hot tub, college savings accounts for my kids, business goals, etc. I read them all every single day. It's that important to me. It needs to be important to you. It's about having a vision.

Remember, life will also have a way of challenging you once you set out to achieve your goal. You will start, and your kids will get sick, or that secure job you had suddenly is not so safe. This is just something you will need to accept as part of the process. It will rain on you. It will be cold at times. People will tell you "no." There will be days you don't feel like showing up and putting in the work. But the quicker you accept and understand it will never be convenient, the quicker you will succeed. Success never goes on sale. Everyone must be willing to pay the price.

You will also have to show up consistently, even when you don't feel like it. These days make it worthwhile, because you will have more days than not when you don't feel like putting in the work. Every single goal and dream is an uphill battle. Don't make decisions based on how you feel. Make them based on life principles like the one I am sharing with you here – the power of having a vision.

My last point is this. If you quit when it gets hard, you guarantee one thing – failure. A Leveled Up Life doesn't consider failure an option. However, if you are willing to push through the challenging times by digging a little deeper internally to find that intestinal fortitude, you will succeed and level up your life. Struggling, my friends, is less painful than regret. Don't ever give up because it got hard. It's hard for everyone. Accept that. Keep on going. I believe your imagination is a preview of life's coming attractions. It was put there for a reason. Seize it.

In summary, if you have a vision for something, it's your job to take the necessary actions to go after it. Believe in yourself. Like I said before, if no one else believes in you, know that I do. You can do this. The key is just to start. Today. Right now.

What's your vision?

CHAPTER 2

FACE YOUR FEARS

"Everything you want is on the other side of fear."
Jack Canfield

rowing up on Long Island meant that you could be at the beach in less than thirty minutes, depending on where you lived. I grew up in Saint James, a hamlet of Smithtown, and could be at the beach on the north shore of Long Island in about ten minutes.

Long Beach and Short Beach were two of the beaches I spent much time at as a kid. They were on the Long Island Sound. They were a little rocky but very big, so it was a great place to be on the weekends. If I ever wanted to go to the ocean, it was about a thirty-minute drive to the south shore of Long Island. We often went to Robert Moses State Park. We were a big Italian family, so my grandparents and cousins would often come along too. I also had two siblings – an older sister and a younger brother. My mother had four siblings, and most of them had kids too. We were a pretty large family and spent much time together.

Around the time I was fifteen years old, I began to envy the lifeguards on the beach. Being in the sun all day, on a beach, and getting paid too was appealing. Also, I was attracted to exciting jobs. The thought of rescuing someone from drowning seemed scary and intense, but, oddly, it also seemed like an enjoyable job.

Since I spent most of my time on the north shore of Long Island, it was the lifeguards on the Long Island Sound I often saw as a kid. They were known technically as "still" water lifeguards, while the lifeguards on the ocean, where there are waves, were known as "open" water lifeguards. Going to the beach sparked my interest to be a still water lifeguard. I had created a vision, like the batting cage, again.

I started my lifeguard journey by taking the American Red Cross Lifeguard training course at Hauppauge High School. Everyone needed to start somewhere, and the entry-level for a lifeguard is a pool lifeguard. You can't just start at the beach. The pool is first, followed by still water, and, if you are good enough, you can train for the open ocean.

As a pool lifeguard, you learn the fundamentals of lifeguarding, culminating in a test in the pool. I didn't have a hard time with this elementary training, and I passed this test my first time. But to work on the beach on the north shore of Long Island, I had to take a different test. The still water test is slightly more challenging, more intense, and more swimming. I failed this exam my first two times. I was devastated. Determined, I knew that I would pass if I simply didn't give up. If I stopped trying, there was only one guarantee, as mentioned in Chapter 1 – failure. That just wasn't an option.

I continued to train, and after taking it the third time, I passed. This test was also given in a pool. I remember one specific scary part of the test that day. The number of kids taking the test and the constant barrage of getting kicked in the face and arms during the long-distance swim portion was brutal. It was like trying to navigate around cars as traffic came at me from both directions. If a candidate stopped for any reason, they

> IF I STOPPED TRYING, THERE WAS ONLY ONE GUARANTEE – FAILURE. THAT JUST WASN'T AN OPTION.

automatically failed. Why? It could be perceived as taking a break and that was not allowed. As I said, I passed the test, and this officially kicked off my lifeguarding career on the beaches of Smithtown, where I grew up. I did this for about three years.

On one of my days off, my family decided to go to the ocean at Robert Moses State Park, which we did often. My grandparents were with us that day. I remember the beach was packed with people. The sun was out, it was around 80°F, with a slight breeze. The sky was blue. It was a picture-perfect day. But there was one big problem. The ocean was rough that day. Very rough. The waves were rolling in one after another. What made it exceptionally dangerous was the riptide. If a big wave knocked you down, it might hurt, but you can get back up most of the time. That day was slightly different. The strong current and riptide could pull you back into the ocean, and when this happened, people often panicked. This is how people drown. That day the lifeguards were constantly jumping off the white lifeguard tower to save someone in the ocean. This went on for what seemed like all day.

Then, something I will never forget happened. My grandfather was sitting to my right, wearing his white beach robe over his bathing suit, which he always wore at the beach. As the lifeguards were rescuing someone for what seemed like the fiftieth time, he said, "David, those are the real lifeguards." Whoa! I didn't expect to hear that. It stung a little bit, but not in a bad way. I took it as a new challenge for myself. A new vision.

I had been a lifeguard for a few years, but it was nothing like ocean lifeguarding. This was on another level. These lifeguards were all in much better shape, and they actually had to save people. Not me. Saving people was something that rarely ever happened at a pool or still water beach.

Fear immediately crept in. I was about five foot eight and 150 pounds soaking wet. I was a good swimmer, but I wasn't that good. I mean, I failed the still water test two times, remember? How could I even think I would pass the open ocean test? I swam on the swim team in high school at the time, but I had some of the worst times. The negative self-talk about making this happen was out of control. I had much fear about it. At the same time, however, I had the drive and vision to go after it. A new vision was born. A new challenge was upon me. But I had fear to overcome – and a lot of it.

First, I needed to find a place I could work as an ocean lifeguard. That was step number one. As kids, we often hear about work through word of mouth, like any kid's job. When I told my parents I wanted to do this, my mother put the word out about my interest in becoming an ocean lifeguard. Sure enough, a close family friend knew the Chief of Lifeguards at Smith Point County Park. She got me an appointment to meet Chief Joseph Dooley.

Smith's Point was an ocean beach in Suffolk County and had the reputation of having some of the best lifeguards around. No one ever drowned there, and that stat still holds today. They were the real deal. Chief Dooley was a legend back in the day and was always known to bring in amazing athletes to work for him. They ran the ocean lifeguard test for all the beaches in the entire county.

I remember meeting Chief Dooley in his office, which was attached to the main clubhouse of the beach. I knocked on the wooden frame screen door, all nervous and scared. He called for me to come in and was already sitting at his desk in the back corner of the room.

I don't remember much of our conversation because I was caught up in the moment. I remember thinking, "Did I really commit to this? There's no way this is going to happen." I don't remember much between my inner voice of fear talking and blankly staring at Chief Dooley. But I do remember how it ended. He said, "David, if you want to be an ocean lifeguard, you need to come back here early, before you go to work, and train with my guys." Umm, what? Come back here before work and train with your guys? Gulp.

"Okay," I responded. I wasn't expecting that challenge, nor was I ready. I questioned myself internally. "What did I just get myself into?"

I showed up that first morning, probably around eight, with permission from my other lifeguarding job to arrive late. I stood around with guys much bigger than me. Or at least that's how I remember it. They either were bigger than me or were athletes of some sort. – local track stars, football players, swimmers, and so on. Not me. I was athletic and all, but these guys were on another level.

I was told their day starts with what they called a "standard" workout. That involved a three-mile run in single file on the beach. All the lifeguards lined up one behind the other for the long jog on the beach. We didn't run near the water where the sand was hard. We ran at the top of the beach, where the sand was soft and much harder to run through. We would try to follow in the tire tracks from the SUVs or police vehicles that drove on the beach, but we didn't always find them. The tire tracks weren't ideal, like running on land, but the sand was firmer. We would go along the beach for a mile and a half. At the halfway point, we would stop and quickly jump in the water to cool off before turning around.

Running back was different. We did a workout that they called, back then, the "Indian Run." In this exercise a team or group of people runs in single file, and the last person in line sprints to the front. When that person gets there, the next person at the end of the line sprints to the front of the queue. We did this back to our starting point. Exhausting. And it didn't end there.

When we finished this part of training, I was directed to look at the buoy floating out in the ocean, about seventy-five yards from shore. It was floating beyond where the waves broke. The head lifeguard told me that we were to sprint into the water when the whistle blew, dive through the waves, swim around the buoy, and swim right back to shore. Once onshore, we must run straight to the back of the beach, up a large dune, around the backside of the dune, and then sprint back to the water to repeat the same process. We did this loop three times. Yes, three. Say what? Should I vomit now? Butterflies were in my stomach just thinking about it. Fear crept in. This "standard' workout was very intense, and to think this was before their workday even started was mind-boggling.

The whistle blew. I remember diving into the water, doing my three loops, and, before I knew it, the standard workout was over. I didn't pass out. I didn't stop or give up. I didn't do that well, but I finished.

I was told to keep coming back by Chief Dooley, and each time I did, I got a little better. On certain days, they additionally practiced ocean rescues. It was much more involved than I knew, and it was an ability I needed to master. The process went by the initials T.V.L.B., which stood for Torpedo, Victim, Line, Beach. Each had its specific role that an open-water lifeguard needed to master because this was the process of rescuing someone.

In addition to training with these lifeguards for weeks, I also trained independently. I swam laps at the pool. I ran. I lifted weights. I did anything I could do to become stronger and more prepared.

The morning of the test finally arrived. I drove to the beach in the Hamptons in my old gray Buick Skyhawk. It wasn't pretty, but it was a gift from my uncle, and it got me around, so I loved it. The warm sun was out, and I had my windows open, enjoying the slight breeze. I was as prepared as I could be. But I had one concern I was praying on. The only thing I wanted that day was for the ocean to be calm. There would be nothing worse than having to take the ocean test on a rough day. The test was the same whether it was rough or super calm. The fear of taking this test with huge waves and possibly a riptide to boot was beyond nauseating.

I pulled into the small beach lot and parked off to my left. As I exited the car, I could feel the breeze blowing directly in my face, as my worst nightmare came true. I could hear the sound of waves crashing on the beach. I couldn't see them, but I could hear them. They were loud. My biggest fear became a reality. My mindset changed quickly, in that instant. Butterflies started in my stomach and fear crept in. I slowly walked towards the check-in table, and I could feel my doubt and fear exponentially increase.

> MY BIGGEST FEAR BECAME A REALITY. MY MINDSET CHANGED QUICKLY, IN THAT INSTANT. BUTTERFLIES STARTED IN MY STOMACH AND FEAR CREPT IN.

When I checked in, they assigned me a number. With a black permanent marker, they wrote a number on the shoulder of both arms so they could identify who I was during the test. After being assigned a number, they paired me with another participant taking the test. Throughout the exam, we often worked with a partner. There was a big group of us that day; there seemed to be about seventy of us. I tried counting everyone when they broke us up in pairs, but I never got an actual count. I just knew there were a lot of us.

As I waited to be paired up with someone, my mind started with the negative self-talk. "Please don't pair me up with someone much bigger than me. I'll fail for certain." As they began pairing us up, my second fear materialized. They paired me up with a guy who looked like Arnold Schwarzenegger. I couldn't believe this was happening. He had muscles popping out of muscles and was probably around six feet tall. First a rough ocean, and now this? Things couldn't get worse, and I was beyond fearful of what was about to happen. I'll refer to this giant of a man as "Arnold" going forward, which appropriately fits.

The first portion of the test was the Cross Chest Carry. In this rescue, the rescuer would swim to their partner/victim who was pretending to drown and roll them onto their back. The rescuer would then put one arm around the victim's chest, and while doing the sidestroke, swim to shore with the victim in tow.

Both partners take on both roles. I played the victim while Arnold rescued me and vice versa. In either case it involved running into the ocean, diving through the waves, and swimming to a buoy offshore about seventy-five yards. There wasn't much break even when you played the victim.

Everyone was assembled along the shoreline and a whistle blew to start the test. The victims sprinted into the water first to get a few seconds' head start. The whistle blew again a few seconds later for the rescuers to sprint to the water to rescue their victims. It looks like you are chasing your victim, but you aren't. Everyone is just scrambling to position to perform their portion of the test. It minimized rest time. The victim should already be at the buoy when the rescuer gets there.

The Cross Chest Carry test begins, and the rescuer swims with the victim towards the shore. This is where it gets tricky and very challenging. When the rescuer gets to an area where they can stand (which is often in the same place where the waves begin to crash), they need to stand up and transition the victim onto their back with the victim's arms slung over the rescuer's shoulders. They are basically carrying the victim on their back. Trying to avoid getting knocked over by a wave, dropping their victim, or having the strength to put their victim on their back is beyond challenging. The goal is to walk the victim out of the water, up the berm of the beach, and ultimately kneel on one knee so the victim can be rolled onto their back. This procedure positions the victim so CPR can be performed if necessary.

I was the rescuer first and had to save and carry Arnold up the beach. I remember getting him on my back, and my only focus was to not drop him. I walked as quickly as possible out of the ocean water and slowly rolled him onto his back. My quads were burning, I was out of breath, water was splashing everywhere from the crashing waves, and I could feel the riptide pulling me back towards the water. It was brutal, but I did it.

As soon as I laid Arnold down, we immediately switched roles, and I was now the victim. I had to sprint back to the water and swim as fast as possible to the buoy. Here's the catch. If you stopped, you failed. If they saw you struggling, you also failed. They watched closely by positioning lifeguards in the water, paddling around on long surfboards. The lifeguards were there to both observe us performing the test but also there to save us if needed. This happened that day to a handful of people taking the test. You can't mess with mother nature, especially the ocean, when it is rough. It overpowered many candidates that day, both mentally and physically.

I remember Arnold swimming up to me for his portion of the Cross Chest Carry. He towed me to the area where he could stand and then needed to transition me onto his back. Large waves continued to crash as he began moving me onto his back. I remember one big wave crashing on us that didn't go well. He dropped me. It wasn't an automatic failure if he dropped me, but he could never let go of me at any point. He got me back up onto his back, but another wave came crashing down, and he dropped me again. He tried a third time, and the same thing happened. After both of us got pummeled by three powerful waves, he threw his hands up in the air and said, "I'm done!" Umm, what?! Arnold just quit? Yes, he did. He was gone. It was that quick.

Within seconds I was paired up with someone else, and the test continued. This went on for about two hours, if I remember correctly. That day I remember eight of us passing – and I was one of those eight! I couldn't believe it. Maybe it was ten. Perhaps it was seven. I don't exactly remember, but the last portion of the test was a written first aid exam, and I remember trying to count everyone that remained quickly. There weren't many of us left. There were so many of us when we started, but that day the ocean won. It defeated many people. It was a day I will never forget.

This is what I learned through all of this. We will never be ready when opportunity knocks. It will never be convenient to go after a goal or dream. We will never wake up one day with extra time, when life isn't throwing some sort of problem at us. We are either in a problem, coming out of a problem, or there is a problem on the horizon tomorrow.

IT WILL NEVER BE CONVENIENT TO GO AFTER A GOAL OR DREAM.

To succeed at anything, sometimes we must avoid the path of least resistance. The more resistance we face, the bigger opportunity for growth. The tension we feel in life is where growth and the real magic happen. On the outer edge of our comfort zones, we level up our life. When Chief Dooley told me that day I needed to start training with his lifeguards, I wasn't ready. I wasn't prepared physically or mentally. Nor was it convenient. I had a job already, and the timing was far from perfect. But I was willing to take that first step forward. When something becomes a priority in our life, we will always find a way to get it done. Otherwise, we find an excuse. This was a priority.

So how did I take that first step? I created a vision and goal for myself that eliminated any sort of hesitation. I followed my intuition. Faith over fear, my friends. Once you find out why you are going after something, you will always find your way. I didn't worry about how I would achieve the goal, but I had to take that first step and lean into all of my fears. Don't worry about figuring out all the puzzle pieces for your life and how you will get there. Just start. The rest will always follow. As mentioned earlier, if you don't at least try, you can guarantee one thing. Failure. Don't be part of that stat.

I like to refer to fear as False Evidence Appearing Real. Ninety-nine percent of the things we worry about never actually happen. When I parked my car and heard the waves crashing on the beach, the fear I had made me anxious. When I was paired with Arnold Schwarzenegger, the fear made my stomach turn. Except, in the end, none of it mattered. I passed, and my partner, who was twice my size, was the one who quit. When you learn to face your fears head on and not worry about all the "what if" scenarios, more times than not, you will succeed. We all have fear. We all have our trials and tribulations in life. We are all human. So give yourself that grace. However, sometimes in life, we need to do what we don't want to do to live the life we want to live. That's a Leveled Up Life.

I had a goal and a dream of being an ocean lifeguard, and I let nothing get in my way. Yes, I had much fear, but I faced it head on. I chose to take action over procrastination.

You, too, have a choice of how you live each day. You cannot control what happens to you, but you can control how you react. You control your actions. You control your decisions. You are where you are right now in life because of the choices and decisions you've made up to this point, and that's okay! But don't wait for things to be perfect to start going after your goals and dreams. That will never happen. Living a Leveled Up Life is about taking action. Be bold and willing to focus forward, taking that first step even when faced with all that fear.

CHAPTER 3

LIFE DOESN'T ALWAYS FIRE A WARNING SHOT

"You don't have to be great to start, but you have to start to be great."

Zig Ziglar

After high school, I attended the University of Albany to get my Bachelor's Degree. It wasn't my first choice by any means. I went to a private Catholic school growing up and graduated from St. Anthony's High School in South Huntington, NY. I would have loved to continue in a private college, but my parents were going through a divorce. The money wasn't there to send me to an expensive private school, so instead, I went to the University of Albany. (I'll discuss more about this later in the book.)

The University of Albany was huge, with close to 20,000 students on campus. I barely knew anyone, but, like most kids, I became friends first with those in my dormitory at school. One night, early in my freshman year, I remember horseplaying around in my dorm room with many other guys. We were wrestling around and, at some point, my head cracked up against the cinderblock wall in my room. It knocked me down and put me in a bad daze. I don't remember much of what happened after that, but I do remember one specific person who came over to help. He brought me ice. His name was David Brinkerhoff. People often called him "Brink." (I often refer to him as "Brink" or "Dave.") Brink helped me with what was probably a concussion that day, and from that point forward we became close friends.

Brink was from western New York, from a town called Boston. He couldn't live any further away from where I grew up on Long Island, which is at the other end of the state. We immediately became great friends and had very similar goals for our future. I knew I wanted to be a police officer by this time, something many people did in my family. My dad was a police officer with the Nassau County Police Department, and my grandfather was part of the Mounted Unit with the New York City Police Department. I didn't want to pursue this profession because of them, but I'm sure being exposed to this line of work piqued my interest as a kid. Brink also wanted to be a police officer, which strengthened the bond and friendship between us. We both loved jobs that were exciting and different and often talked about all the police exams we wanted to take.

Because the University of Albany was so big, it had its own Volunteer Ambulance Corps called "Five Quad Ambulance." It was composed of students who were also Emergency Medical Technicians (EMTs). Brink and I were interested in doing this together. He joined right away since he was already an EMT. I wasn't, so I had to go through all the training, but I took the EMT courses and got certified too. A typical shift on the ambulance required one driver and two EMTs. However, when Brink and I saw some additional training that allowed just two people to ride per shift, we pursued that too. We used to work the midnight shifts together, responding to calls, hanging out, and just building a very good friendship.

I also worked at Macy's during this time because, as mentioned earlier, my parents were divorced, so money was often tight. I worked in the women's shoe department (yes, women's shoes because the commission was great!) to start out and ultimately transitioned into the security department. This was a lot more fun and exciting than selling shoes, plus it aligned with my future in law enforcement. Brink also wanted a job during college, and I was able to get him into the security department. Whether we were volunteering at Five Quad Ambulance or working at Macy's, we truly became the best of friends.

In our sophomore year Dave and I became dorm roommates and started talking about pledging a fraternity. We both looked at the different fraternities on campus,

CONTINUALLY LOOKING FOR OPPORTUNITIES – SMALL AND LARGE – MOVED ME CLOSER AND CLOSER TO MY GOALS.

and both had an interest in the same one – Sigma Alpha Mu, aka "Sammy." This was the fraternity that we expressed interest in, and not surprisingly, we were both accepted into this brotherhood. After our sophomore year, Brink and I moved into Sigma Alpha Mu house in Albany and lived with a few other brothers. Brink was hands down my best friend during my college years, and we pretty much did everything together.

When the New York State Police Entrance Exam was given, we decided to take the first portion of the test, the written exam. We were juniors at the time but learned that if you wanted to be a police officer, you needed to start taking the tests years in advance. The processing took a while, so starting at a young age was important. At no surprise to anyone, we both scored within a few tenths of a point of each other on the written exam. We both attained a ninety-eight point something and were called to the second phase of testing simultaneously. This second stage was the physical fitness portion, followed by a lengthy written psychological exam.

In the fall of our senior year, we received acceptance letters from the New York State Police and were invited to the Academy class beginning in November. Not only did we both get into the same class, but we both would have to leave college early. Because this was our dream, we accepted the positions without hesitation and entered the State Police Academy on November 2, 1998. It was a grueling six months of training and living at the Academy, but we both graduated as New York State Troopers.

We didn't end up being assigned to the same area of the state upon graduation, but we remained best friends.

Brink was assigned to the Albany area and met his wife, Barbara, who was a Registered Nurse at a hospital. I, too, met my wife Kristen when I worked in Westchester County. Brink and I ended up getting married around the same time and were both in each other's weddings. We remained best friends and were always instrumental in each other's lives.

During our time with the State Police, Brink and I had goals and aspirations of being on the SWAT Team. It would bring another level of excitement and something we both strived to achieve. At the time, it was called the Mobile Response Team (MRT). The first time tryouts were offered, I wasn't selected, and Brink wasn't eligible. His semi-annual firearm training scores weren't where they needed to be to qualify. The second time it rolled around, in 2006, I had been promoted to Investigator in the State Police, which is their detective division. It was called the Bureau of Criminal Investigation (BCI). As an Investigator, you are not eligible to try out for the MRT. Brink was still a Trooper and ultimately was allowed to try out. He made the team, and I couldn't have been happier for him. It was something he always wanted.

Brink's wife, Barbara (often called Barb) was pregnant around that time and gave birth to their daughter Isabella. Brink called me after she was born to let me know that Isabella had Down syndrome and Barb wasn't doing well after the labor. As hard as that must have been for Brink, he always remained positive about his daughter's condition and was optimistic about Barb making a full recovery.

On April 24, 2007, New York State Trooper Matthew Gombosi was shot in Margaretville, NY, by Travis Trim.

Trooper Gombosi was dispatched to a call of a suspicious male in the parking lot of a gas station minimart. When Trooper Gombosi arrived and approached Trim, he pulled out a handgun and shot Trooper Gombosi in the chest. Trooper Gombosi's bulletproof vest stopped the bullet, and he survived with just minor injuries. Trooper Gombosi didn't know that Travis Trim had a warrant out for his arrest from the Probation Department. Trim immediately fled the area, resulting in a massive manhunt to capture him.

The New York State Police called the MRT to assist with the search, which involved Brink as he was a member of MRT. I was still an Investigator and heard about the shooting in Margaretville, but it was hours away from me, so I didn't have specific details.

On the morning of April 25, 2007, I was sitting at my desk at the BCI office of the Cortlandt Barracks. It was a large room that included five other Investigators' desks. We got word that another State Trooper was shot and that it was an MRT member. I remember jumping out of my desk, walking outside, and frantically calling Brink, trying to get in touch with him. The phone rang and rang, and he never picked up. I left multiple voicemail messages.

"Brink, it's Dave. I heard an MRT member was shot. Call me back."

I then called again, a little more concerned.

"Brink! Where are you? Call me back! An MRT member was shot. What is going on?"

Then again, I called.

"Brink, me again! Trying to get in touch with you. An MRT member was shot. Call me back!"

After numerous failed attempts to get in touch with Brink, I walked back into my office and sat at my desk. Our general office phone rang, and my friend Paul Schneeloch, a fellow Investigator, answered it. Paul was sitting directly in front of me, slightly off to my right. My desk faced the side of Paul's desk, so we made eye contact as Paul said, "Dave, a guy by the name of Adam is on the phone for you. He said he knows you from college and is asking to speak to you?"

I said to myself, "Adam? I worked at Macy's with an Adam. Why is he calling?"

I picked up the phone and said, "Hello."

"Dave, it's Adam."

"Hey, Adam what's going on?"

"Did you hear about the Trooper that was shot?"

"Yeah, I did. I've been trying to get in touch with Brink."

I began telling Adam how I was leaving multiple messages for Brink, and he interrupted me, cutting me off, "Dave, it was Brink."

"Wait, what? Is he okay?"

"No."

"What do you mean, no?

"He didn't make it."

April 25, 2007, I lost my best friend. It was the worst day of my life. Dave was in a tragic shootout with Travis Trim inside a residence he broke into to hide from police. When the house alarm went off, the MRT was called in to search the house. As they got to the second floor, it turned into a fierce gunfight. Trooper Richard Mattson, aka Mad Dog, also sustained a career-ending gunshot wound to his arm. It was a devastating day for the New York State

Police, and Travis Trim was shot by Brink during the gunfight. Right before Brink was mortally wounded, he pulled the trigger hitting Trim in the head, ultimately killing him. My best friend left this earth a hero – a hero who may have saved other lives.

After my friend Adam told me about Brink, I immediately began sobbing at my desk, so hard it hurt. My boss at the time, Bruce Cuccia, walked out of his office, and came up from behind me to put his hand on my right shoulder and began squeezing it. After a moment or two, I got up and walked out the door behind me, and went outside. I called my mother and father to tell them. They were some of the most challenging phone calls I'd had to make. I cried while telling them.

"Hello, Dad! It's me." My dad was playing golf at the time when I told him. He was about to ask me to hold on, but I interrupted him and said, "Dad, it's an emergency!"

He said, "Oh, okay. What's up?"

"Brink got shot upstate, and he didn't make it. They were trying to catch a guy that shot a Trooper yesterday, and the MRT Team was involved. He didn't make it. Brink died! I lost my best friend!"

It was brutal. When I walked back inside and sat at my desk, my good friend Paul leaped up from his desk, walked over to me, grabbed me by the shoulder, and said "Let's go." He turned to our boss, Bruce, "We are going to the hospital where Brink is."

The drive up to this hospital was an absolute blur. Paul drove with the lights and sirens on to get there quickly while I frantically tried to get more information on the phone. My friend Norville, an MRT member with Brink, was also there. I was able to get him on the phone. He was with Brink during the incident. I cried and asked him, "What happened?!"

Norville was crying out loud, and the only response he could muster, which was hard to understand, was "I tried my best! I tried my best!" The crying and Norville repeatedly saying, "I tried my best," will stick with me for the rest of my life.

We arrived at the hospital, and all you could make out was a sea of blue. As far as the eyes could see were State Trooper and other police vehicles. I jumped out of the car and walked directly through the emergency room doors, past many other people. Everyone was huddled close together, crying. No one stopped me as I was walked right into the emergency room. It was as if they knew I was Brink's best friend. I remember asking random people, "Where is Brink? Where is he? What room is he in?"

Finally, I came to a door where an Investigator I didn't know was standing guard at the door. I said again, "Where is Brink?"

He motioned to the door behind me and stepped to the side, so I walked right in. Brink was lying on a stretcher covered from the chest down with a sheet. His shoulders and face were exposed. I wailed, "BRRRIIINNNNKKKK! OH, GOD! BRRRRIIIINNNNKKK!"

He was lifeless, just lying there. He didn't even look injured, which made matters worse. It was as if he was sleeping. I fell to my knees with my hands over his body and cried endlessly.

As I write I'm in tears sharing this story with you. It touched me in a way I will never forget. Dave impacted my life in ways no one else ever has. We did everything together. From college, to work, to our weddings, to the State Police, and everything in between.

A few days earlier, we had talked on the phone as I was driving home. I remember exactly where I turned onto my neighborhood block when we finished the call. We talked about the family trip we planned together to the Outer Banks, South Carolina. I remember telling him my check for the vacation was in the mail (he organized it), and he jokingly responded, "It better not be made out of rubber."

That was the last conversation I ever had with Dave. We hung up, and little did I know what was about to happen.

When I walked out of Brink's hospital room, I looked to my left and saw Dave's mom, Karen, walking slowly around the corner. She turned towards me, made eye contact, and cried out "David!" She ran toward me, hugging and crying on my shoulder. I took Karen in to see Dave for the first time, and those heavy tears of emotion fell all over again. I will never forget Karen crying out, "Oh, David! Oh, David." I didn't know what to do. I just stood there for support.

Dave's father and brothers arrived as well. My wife Kristen was picked up from work by a State Trooper and also arrived at the hospital. I took Kristen in to see Dave, and it was another challenging moment for us – one I will never forget. Kristen stood to my right, holding my hand near the foot of the bed, staring at Dave. Tears were coming down her face. Not many words were shared, but I kept saying repeatedly, "He's gone. He's gone." My best friend was gone. Forever.

Dave's wife, Barb, was in a private room for the family. I kept going in and out of the room to comfort her. Any conversation was minimal. There was nothing anyone could say to ease the pain. Many people simply cried and sat in silence. That was the only support anyone could give. The mere presence of people together was consoling, so that's what we did.

What I found out a few days later made all these events even harder. The investigation of the incident revealed that Brink was killed by friendly fire. During the gunfight, my friend Norville, whom I spoke about earlier, was standing right behind Brink during the shootout. He accidentally clipped Brink in the back of the head through his helmet. Brink was shot a few seconds earlier in the chest by Travis Trim, but his vest caught it. Even after taking one shot to the chest, he stayed in the gunfight. Brink took a knee during the gunfight, and Norville was standing right behind him. As Brink tried to stand up and go towards Trim, he was struck by Norville. Like I said earlier, Brink died a hero that day and what happened with Norville was an absolute tragedy.

People often ask me if I blame Norville. The answer is unequivocally, "No." Travis Trim caused this incident and was actively shooting at the MRT Troopers. Norville was doing his best in the situation he was in. Nothing good came of this incident. Lives were lost. Careers ended, and the mental trauma so many of us had to deal with still affects us today.

I learned something very powerful from this tragedy – a principle

LIFE DOESN'T ALWAYS FIRE A WARNING SHOT.

I practice every day. My friends, life doesn't always fire a warning shot. So many of us talk about all the things that we are going to do. We wait to have extra time or extra money. We wait to be less busy. We wait for things to be perfect. We wait for it to be more convenient. But the fact of the matter is that reality doesn't exist. It will never happen. We will never have extra money or extra time. We will never wake up with an abundance of time one day. We will always be busy. Time never stops and, before you know it, yesterday is in the past and we must understand that tomorrow is not guaranteed. We only have today. After losing Brink I learned in an instant that we may not be here tomorrow. Life can be taken from us that quickly.

Like I mentioned earlier the wealthiest place on earth is the graveyard. It is full of goals, ideas, and dreams never acted upon. Don't become part of that stat. When I lost Brink, a significant shift in my mindset and how I live my life each day changed.

God's gift to us is potential, and our gift back is what we do with it. What potential do you have that you aren't acting on because you think tomorrow is guaranteed? What goals are you sitting on because you are waiting to be less busy? What potential do you have that you are leaving untapped because of excuses?

Every day I live life with a sense of urgency. Every day I refuse to allow myself to become a victim and blame others for my lack of success in life. I wake up with the intention to move forward and take ownership of the day. I control my time. I control my hours. I control my days and, ultimately, I control my life.

To think that life will get easier is a myth. If we want things to change, we need to change. If we want the next thirty days to not look like the last thirty, the only thing that needs to change is us. Instead of wishing life would be easier, we must be willing to get better. It's on us as individuals to be the change we want to see and stop waiting for someone else to rescue us.

As quick as Brink lost his life, we can lose ours too. So sitting around waiting for things to line up perfectly is not a good plan. I don't know what goals or dreams you have right now, but I know you have some. We are all human, and we all dream. Maybe they are buried deep inside you because you've allowed all your excuses to creep in for years. But I'm here to tell you they are still there. You just need to peel back all the layers of excuses like an onion and find that dream or goal you once had. If you are looking for a sign to act upon it, maybe this is it.

I am begging you right now – today – go out there and go after those goals and dreams you once had. Don't wait for other people to support you. Don't wait for someone to encourage you to start. The only person needed to support your goals and dreams is the one you see in the mirror every single day. That is you!

Go out there and live your life as if this may be your last day. You deserve to live a life of excellence. But it will require a victor mentality, not a victim mentality. The Leveled Up Life requires us to have the mindset of a victor. Make today the day you draw a line in the sand to make that change. It's a decision and something you have complete control over. There are 86,400 seconds in a day. Use them wisely to live your life to its fullest potential.

CHAPTER 4

GROWTH COMES FROM ADVERSITY

"I hated every minute of training, but I said, 'Don't quit. Suffer now and live the rest of your life as a champion.'"

Muhammad Ali

By 2010 my wife Kristen and I were both well into our careers. She was an elementary school teacher, and I was an Investigator with the Bureau of Criminal Investigation. We had two daughters at the time, and we quickly fell into the trap of having a "busy life."

You know the drill. Wake up, rush around all morning to get yourselves and the kids ready, take them to daycare, and rush into work. Then as soon as you got home, it was a rush to eat dinner, handle all the kids' activities for that day, and then face what I like to call the "witching hours." Those were the hours at night when the kitchen needed to be straightened up from dinner, the girls needed to take baths and get ready for bed, and then we needed to get ourselves situated and prepared for the next day. What made it more difficult (parents, you will relate) was how tired and cranky the kids often were after a long day. Their level of cooperation at night was often pretty minimal. We would go to bed exhausted and repeat the same process every day. I know many of you can relate. It often felt like we were on the merry-go-round of life.

We struggled in a few other areas as well. We weren't in the best place financially. We both made six figures in our careers, but we fell into the same trap so many of us do. As we make more money, we spend more. We didn't have a savings account, and, more times than not, we simply lived paycheck to paycheck.

Our health also took a backseat. I was about twenty-five pounds heavier than I wanted to be, and Kristen struggled to lose the baby weight she gained from having kids. I had a gym membership but didn't get there as often as I liked because of being a busy dad. Also, I had been a runner and ran the New York City Marathon twice, but I didn't have time anymore for something like this. Overall it wasn't that we weren't grateful for where we were in life, but I often asked myself, "Is this it? Is this what life is supposed to look like? Work a job, come home, take care of the kids, go to bed and repeat the same process every day?" I knew something needed to change.

The problem was finding the time. As we all say, "I don't have the time to add anything else to my plate." The answer was simple. It came through our priorities. If we wanted our lives to change, we needed to change. We only get twenty-four hours in a day. The difference between successful people and those who aren't isn't that they have more time; it's that they manage their time more effectively.

Around the same time, my co-worker was endeavoring to get me to try a fitness program called "P90X." He even dropped the DVDs on my desk. They sat there for months collecting dust. I told him I wouldn't do workouts on DVDs. I was a runner and gym goer. I didn't need a home workout and, quite honestly, I didn't believe I would get results.

A few months went by and the two of us were sent to Houston, Texas, to look for the witness to a homicide case that just occurred in New York. We found our witness and finished the day a little early. As you already know I am a big baseball fan and I asked my colleague if he wanted to go to the Houston Astros baseball game. He agreed but said I needed to do the sixteen-minute ab workout of P90X first, back at the hotel room, in order for him to go. I reluctantly agreed and to my surprise I could barely finish. I woke up the next day beyond sore. Little did I know at the time I was finding a solution to the problem of not having the time to get to the gym.

So, Kristen and I decided to start getting up a little earlier each morning to work out at home for an hour, using the P90X DVDs. This meant getting up before our kids woke up. We knew that life would always get

> TO SUCCEED AT ANYTHING, SACRIFICES HAVE TO BE MADE.

in the way if we tried to exercise after work or late at night. It required sacrifices like giving up a little sleep. To succeed at anything, sacrifices have to be made.

Was this easy? Not at all. Who wants to get up earlier and out of a warm bed? No one. But our priorities shifted, and once something becomes a priority in your life, you always find a way to get it done. Otherwise, we find an excuse. We wanted to go from just surviving in life to actually thriving.

What started happening was quite interesting. Not only did we start losing weight and become healthier, we also started feeling much better mentally. We were less stressed. We had more energy. We were getting more done in a day because we were more effective with the energy we gained from daily exercise. Getting up early didn't cost us time. It bought us time back. We became better parents, better spouses, better employees, and overall were better with anything we touched or got ourselves involved in. I strongly feel our kids deserve the best of us, not what's left of us.

People noticed the difference in us, and we started sharing what we were doing from home. It was a very natural process. People asked. We shared what we did and sent them directly to the company website to purchase the programs from them. This started with a few people, and then it continued to grow. At this point we learned we could earn income from sharing what we were doing with others, so we decided to sign up with the company as independent distributors. We didn't know that we were actually sitting on a big business, but we were. We just thought if we could make a few extra dollars to make a car payment we would be happy. Once we began to see other people succeed in the same company at a very high level, we decided to pursue it for ourselves in earnest.

But here's what happened. Once we started actively building a secondary income in the online business space, the haters and naysayers came out. People mocked what we did. They said it wasn't a real job. People laughed at us. People told us it wouldn't last or wouldn't work. The hardest part was that the majority of people who gave us the most criticism were our close friends, family, and co-workers. It just seems to be a fact of life that the people closest to you are often the ones who will criticize you for what you do.

This is what we learned. When you try to separate yourself from the norm, people will hate on you. People will always make comments and snicker. But you need to learn to bless and release them. If you have a vision of doing something, then go for it. Block out the noise, and don't let others tell you what to do with your life. God put this vision inside of your imagination, not inside someone else's.

On the flip side, you will never be criticized by someone more successful than you, no matter what you are trying to accomplish. I'm willing to bet that those who want to tell you something won't work never did it themselves. More times than not, people base their criticism on their reality and what they experienced in their own lives. You are different. It's nobody else's job to support your goals or dreams but you. You will find that if you are willing to push through the pain, many of your naysayers and critics will come around and support you. This happened to my wife and me when we successfully built a big business as distributors. The key is that you cannot stop. The struggle is less painful than regret. Don't ever

> **THE STRUGGLE IS LESS PAINFUL THAN REGRET.**

stop because of what others say. Other people's opinions of you are not your reality.

In the end, this is your life. You need to create the life *you* want for yourself and not create the life others try to pigeonhole you into. There is one crucial thing you need to remember. Growth comes from facing adversity. It comes from constantly being challenged. You must be willing to grow as a person and face the challenges, critics, and obstacles along the way.

My favorite author, John C. Maxwell, says, "Everything worthwhile is uphill." This couldn't be more accurate. If you want something you never had, you need to be willing to do something you've never done. This will require you to leave your comfort zones of life because growth and success will only happen when you stretch yourself.

People often ask me how I overcame all this adversity initially. The answer was simple and still holds true today. I wholly commit each day to surrounding myself with those who are more successful than me and study what they do. Find someone who has what you want and do what they do. How did I find them? Through books. I committed myself to a personal growth journey and I read or listen to at least one book a month to help me grow as a person and change how I think for the better.

Your brain is a muscle. If you put garbage in, garbage will come out. If you wake up every day and use the news to train your brain muscles, you will live in constant stress, anger, and disappointment. Think about it. What do you see when you turn on the news or read the newspaper? You see death, trauma, ugly politics, hate, and much more negativity. Does this serve you in helping you grow and succeed? Absolutely not!

Remember, the news is a business, and it's always sensationalized because it captures the general public's attention. How often do you see stories of positivity, success, and all the good this world offers? Rarely. You don't because it doesn't sell like the shock and awe that death and trauma does. I limit my daily news intake, so I know enough of what's going on in the world around me to be in tune with society. I'm not saying you need to stay oblivious to the world but what I am saying is that your consumption of news media can be stopping you from living the life you want to live.

So how did I find the time to do this? I commit to ten-minute reading pockets throughout my day – right before bed, as soon as I get up, during lunch, etc. I also turned my car into a mobile university. I listen to books on audio when driving to and from work. Rather than listening to the news or music on my commute, I fuel my mind with something that will serve me. Again we all have the time. It's how we manage our time that's the difference.

Everything I shared above doesn't come easy. But if we want things to change for the better, we cannot wait for others to do it for us. We can't wait for someone to rescue us. We need to be our own heroes and start making the changes in our lives. Small incremental changes every day compounded over time lead to massive success.

Success doesn't happen overnight. It happens by leaning into the adversity of life and being intentional every day to do the things that will move your life forward.

That's living a Leveled Up Life. You control the choices and decisions you make every day. No one else does. Choose to do the things that serve you. If it's not helping you, it's time to cut it out of your life. Live the life you deserve to live and start being your own hero. Make that change today.

PART TWO

EXECUTING THE PRINCIPLES

CHAPTER 5

IT'S BIGGER
THAN YOU

*"Only those who have learned the power of
sincere and selfless contribution experience
life's deepest joy: true fulfillment."*

Tony Robbins

When we are kids, everything we do is for ourselves for the most part. We live each day not having to worry about anything or anyone. When we are hungry or need something, we are only concerned with ourselves. These one-way decisions often don't affect anyone other than ourselves at that young age.

But as we get older, the choices and decisions we make each day impact other people. What we do or don't do can directly bear on someone else's life, whether business decisions at work or parental choices at home. Our choices and how we live 100 percent of the time will affect someone else. Many don't realize that people will never forget how you treated them or how you made them feel. Is there someone who impacted you personally, in either a positive or negative way? You may not know the house they lived in or the car they drove, but you will never forget how they made you feel.

We would expect that selfishness will dissipate with age, as we reach adulthood, but that's not the case. We are always thinking about ourselves. Author John C. Maxwell once said, "Who is the first person you look at in a photo after taking a picture with someone?" Exactly. It's ourselves. Even as grown adults, we still think in a way that puts ourselves first.

But herein lies the problem. Except for a tiny speck on this earth, the world is composed of people other than you. If you want to succeed in life, you have to flip your mindset from me to we because there are many people in this world other than you. Each day you must strive to have a positive impact both at work *and* home. There is nothing worse than being a public success and a private failure. Meaning you are succeeding at the highest level at work, but your marriage is in disarray at home, or you aren't there for your kids being the parent and role model they need.

> **IF YOU WANT TO SUCCEED IN LIFE, YOU HAVE TO FLIP YOUR MINDSET FROM ME TO WE BECAUSE THERE ARE MANY PEOPLE IN THIS WORLD OTHER THAN YOU.**

LIKE FATHER, LIKE DAUGHTER

At six years of age, my daughter Sadie began asking my wife Kristen and me if she could play ice hockey.

My wife and I never played this sport growing up, and other than watching some of my friends play it in high school, I knew nothing about it. I didn't know about the equipment that was needed, where to play, how the season worked, anything. Because I never played it myself, being able to teach her seemed impossible.

One morning Kristen and I were in the kitchen talking about Sadie and her continued desire to play ice hockey again. What should we do? Keep saying no or look into this? She was eight years old now, so two years had gone by since she started asking us to play. As we discussed this dilemma, out of the corner of our eyes we saw Sadie in the driveway. She was dragging her plastic hockey net she received for her birthday down the driveway. It was about 20°F on that cold winter morning. After she'd put the net in place, she began shooting her ball into it. She used the plastic hockey stick she also got for her birthday and continued taking shots in the cold temperatures. At that moment, we knew we had to look into it.

We signed Sadie up for a one-day ice hockey clinic to see if she liked it. We weren't anticipating much. I wasn't there, but Kristen explained how she crawled out onto the ice. She could barely stand up, and many of the kids on the ice were way ahead of her because they came from hockey families. Not us. We knew nothing. When the clinic ended, Kristen expected Sadie to come off the ice and tell her she didn't like it. It was the exact opposite. When Kristen asked her, "What did you think?" Her answer was, "I loved it!" We weren't picturing that response. She even said she wanted to keep playing.

We signed Sadie up to play on a team right away, and she went on to play primarily with boys. She worked very hard from the beginning, more than we could ever have imagined. She pushed herself to get better each day, and no matter how many times she fell, she kept getting back up. We hadn't seen any of this coming.

YOUR CHILDREN ARE WATCHING

What we didn't know was that Sadie was watching everything Kristen and I did when it came to pursuing our goals and dreams as we began building our business. She witnessed how we made sacrifices every day going after our dreams, how we had a strong work ethic, and how we were determined to succeed while taking complete ownership of our success. The list went on and on, but this was what we learned. Our kids will often ignore what we say, but they will watch everything we do. Sadie took what she saw in my wife and me and began applying it to her ice hockey life.

When I deliver the keynote at speaking events I frequently share a video of my daughter's journey. I recorded her during her early years and asked her questions about hustle, adversity, and working hard. She talked about pushing herself, getting stronger, and persevering to achieve first place. The last question I asked her was, "Why do we never give up?" She responded, "Because we are the Atkins' family." I didn't expect that answer, and it was a much more powerful response than I anticipated.

Kristen and I never spoke about any of this or what we did. She just observed our behavior and actions and applied it to her own life. Today, after six years with the boys, Sadie is now playing on an all-girls elite ice hockey team in Connecticut with the goals and aspirations of playing Division I in college. As I write this Chapter, I am on a plane from New York to Nashville, Tennessee, for an NHL Elite girls' tournament. The story of my daughter's future is to be continued.

DON'T LET QUITTING BE YOUR LEGACY

As adults, when we give up on ourselves too soon, we often don't know the negative impression we may make on those closest to us, like our kids. They see us talk about what we are going to do but then see us give up on ourselves far too early. We may not even realize that our kids watch us this closely. But they do, and it's either affecting them positively or negatively.

Too many of us, when pursuing something, don't realize the price that has to be paid to achieve success and, therefore, often give up. But quitting doesn't affect you only. Later in life, when you get married or have kids, it will affect those closest to you. Is giving up what you want those closest to you to see? Is that the legacy you want to leave behind for generations to come? I know the answer for all of you is no. You must remember that life is bigger than just you, and you need to understand that.

> THE SPEED OF THE LEADER IS THE SPEED OF THE PACK.

During my last three-and-a-half years with the New York State Police, I was a Captain in charge of all State

Police operations for the entire County of Westchester, New York. Our dispatch center handled approximately four- to five-hundred thousand 911 calls a year. I had about one hundred personnel under my command, from State Troopers to Sergeants to Lieutenants to dispatchers. It was a very busy place. The New York State Police is a paramilitary organization, as it should be for a profession as dangerous as this.

The men and women working for you need to take orders and fulfill them without question in any emergency. You cannot afford to tell someone to do something and have resistance or questioning. An order needs to be obeyed, or you can face consequences, such as a suspension or termination for being insubordinate.

But this is what I learned. When you go out of your way to put people first and show them you care, they will give you 1000 percent more effort when you need something. I didn't want my people to do what I asked of them because they didn't have a choice. I wanted them to do it because they wanted to and do it better than I asked. I didn't want to be the kind of Captain that when I entered the room, everyone snapped to attention, saluted me, and quickly scurried out. I wanted to be the Captain that had their respect and, at the same time, the Captain my people knew had their backs and cared about them.

How did this happen? Putting them first. I would often take the time to learn more about my Troopers and their families. I would stop in the halls to ask people how they were doing. I would go to my Sergeants' and Lieutenants' offices to talk about everyday life. I would stop in the barracks and talk to my Troopers in their main area, called "the squad room." Do you know what happened, then? Productivity went up. They often went above and beyond in all areas of their performance. They were happy. I was pleased, and the world was a better – and safer – place for it.

Friends, life is so much bigger than you. The choices and decisions you make every day will impact your life forever. Your kids and those closest to you will watch what you do, not what you say. They, in turn, will go out and live their life based on what they see from you. Stop quitting. Stop giving up when it gets hard. Stop complaining about why you didn't get this or why you didn't get that. Instead, take full ownership of your life and start taking massive action towards your goals. Yes, it will be hard. No, it won't be easy. Yes, it will test your willpower and perseverance. But it will be worth it! It's the Leveled Up Life!

Start recognizing that life is bigger than just you and use that as an anchor and driving force to press forward. Use that as the fortitude you need each day to push through those hard times. Use it as the urgency and grit you need to be that role model for those you love most.

This is how you leave a legacy. This is how you impact the generations after you. Leading by example and putting people first. The speed of the leader is the speed of the pack. Leave this earth better than you found it. Put others first in all that you do and choose to accept the hard work it will take to get there. Motivational speaker and prolific author, Zig Ziglar once said, "Help enough people get what they want, and you will get what you want." Live by that quote. Live your life this way and watch how much further you get in life and how much better you feel about it. There is no better feeling than helping someone else and no better way to do it than leading by example. The world is a better place, and you will accomplish more than you could ever imagine.

CHAPTER 6

NO EXCUSES

"Excuses are well planned lies."

Dani Johnson

I see it all the time. People are excited and fired up about their new goals, and in a matter of weeks excuses creep in and we give up. Why is this? Why do we give up so easily? Why do people set goals for themselves only to set them aside a few weeks later?

We see this most frequently around the New Year. People set goals to lose weight, and everyone is giving 100 percent on January 2. But in a matter of weeks, it's back to our same old ways, and the crowded gyms empty. Or maybe we are excited about our new business venture, telling the world about it, but when it starts to get hard, we start blaming society, the economy, or other people for why it didn't work.

EXCUSES CHANGE OUR MINDSET

There is nothing more draining than hearing excuses. It's wearing to the person who hears them, but it's even more exhausting to the person making them. And one of the principles I live by is to not make excuses – to others or to myself.

We don't realize that by continuing to make excuses, it trains our minds to believe that these excuses are actually valid when they're not. Excuses often lead us down a path of blaming everyone but ourselves for why we aren't successful. Through my years of building a business, keynote speaking, or even when I was a New York State Trooper, I heard every excuse in the book.

When I was a Trooper, I would often run radar for people speeding. When I stopped them and approached their vehicle, I always asked the driver if they knew why they were getting pulled over. Let me start by saying this: 98 percent of the time people know why they are getting pulled over, but instead of admitting it, they'd say, "No, I don't. I have no idea." Rather than admit they were going 81 mph, they think that, by some slight chance, the Trooper has no clue. They feel that lying or denying their speed will work out for the better. It never does.

For me, people who admitted their wrongdoing and subsequently apologized often got a break because of their honesty. But many wouldn't admit this, so then came the excuses. "I need to go to the bathroom. I was just keeping up with traffic. The car in front of me was going faster than I was." I heard them all. Excuse after excuse.

DEBUNKING THE PLETHORA OF EXCUSES

Author and speaker Dani Johnson said, "Excuses are well planned lies." This couldn't be stated any better. Let me start with the number one excuse. People regularly talk about how *busy* they are and their lack of time. The busy excuse is something that everyone wears as if it were a badge of honor. It's not. It's not serving you.

Everyone is busy. Everyone is dealing with life's problems. Everyone has issues. Everyone deals with sickness or death. Everyone is struggling at one point in their career. Everyone has problems with their kids. Everyone is busy with life. But we all have the same twenty-four hours in a day. The difference between those who are successful and those who aren't has nothing to do with one person being less busy than another. It has everything to do with how the successful person manages their time and their attitude towards it.

Successful people manage their time wisely. It's that simple. They reverse engineer their years, months, weeks, and days. They set their priorities, take complete ownership of their schedule, and don't allow the word "busy" to become an excuse. For example, I look at my calendar each week to see all the activities that need my attention. Family activities, work appointments, etc. Then, for whatever goals I set for myself, I schedule in the time to focus on just that. About eleven years ago, taking care of my health became a priority, as mentioned earlier. My kids were very young, and my wife and I worked full time. We looked at our "busy" schedule just like everyone else and realized that to get in our daily exercise, we needed to get up extra early, around five in the morning, before our kids got up. We didn't make the excuse of not having enough time. We made the time. We scheduled it in. We took ownership of our life and didn't allow our excuses to stop us. We all are handed 86,400 seconds in a day. No more, no less. Something you saw from me earlier, but it bears repeating. It's what you do with your time that makes the difference.

> THERE ARE 86,400 SECONDS IN A DAY. NO MORE. NO LESS. IT'S WHAT YOU DO WITH YOUR TIME THAT MAKES THE DIFFERENCE.

Where you are right now in your life is a product of the choices and decisions you made up until this point. You have a choice every single day with the actions you take. No one controls that but you. Busy is not an excuse, so you need to stop making it one. There are people right now in worse situations and busier than you crushing their goals. Stop using it as an excuse. If you set a goal to achieve something, you need to prioritize it. When something is a priority, you will always find a way. Otherwise, you find an excuse.

We also play the *blame game* and blame others for our lack of success. Let me remind you that life will be a dog fight, my friends. Whenever you set out to achieve something, life always has a funny way of throwing curveballs. Blaming others for your lack of success is not an excuse. When you blame someone else for your lack of success, you give them power over your life. This gets you nowhere. It's easy to blame someone or something rather than take ownership of your life.

Successful people face similar trials and tribulations like everyone else, but they take 100-percent ownership of their lives. If some obstacle comes their way, which they always do, they make the necessary adjustments and move forward. If someone tells them no, they keep going until they get that yes. If someone quits on them, they find someone else to help them. If their mother or father wasn't there or didn't support them, they press forward. They never pass blame.

There was a time when I was building my business that I waited around for someone to support me. I used to wait for someone to tell me what to do. I waited for someone or something to free me so I could succeed. This went on for a while until one day I realized I needed to free myself. I needed to let go of holding myself hostage from achieving success by blaming others. Taking full ownership of my life was freeing and gave me the power to move forward. The same energy I used each day to blame others, I turned around and used to work harder on myself, taking possession of my life. If I failed, it was on me. I also knew that it was also on me if I did succeed. I was entirely responsible for my life. Blaming others will get you nowhere, so stop doing it.

We cannot wake up each day playing the *victim card* either. People live each day complaining about everything that has happened to them. "Why did this happen to me?" or "Why did that happen?" As I stated above, there are people in worse situations than you succeeding at the highest levels in life. How? They don't play the victim card, and they don't blame others.

We are all handed problems in life. We are all facing

trials and tribulations. But how you respond to your situation is the critical difference. Your attitude is the determining factor. You control your attitude daily. Accept it and choose to answer with the right attitude when something unexpected happens. Don't play the victim card as if a particular situation has only happened to you. It's happened to all of us. Choose to react in a way that will serve you for the better.

My wife and I give ourselves twenty-four hours to deal with something negative. We get twenty-four hours to have our pity party but then it's over. We refuse to go on for days complaining or whining about what happened. We need to brush ourselves off and get back on the saddle. The victim mentality never serves you for the better. Instead, you must shift your thinking from a victim mentality to a victor mentality.

SHIFT YOUR THINKING FROM A VICTIM MENTALITY TO A VICTOR MENTALITY.

Justifying our excuses is another path that leads us nowhere. This happens when we take all of our excuses and start using them to justify why we didn't succeed. At the end of the day, the only person we are cheating and letting down is ourselves. People are so caught up in their own life problems that they don't care about yours. I know that's harsh, but it's the truth. I know we feel the need to justify to someone else why something didn't work out, but honestly, deep down, that person doesn't care. Everyone is struggling with their life problems. So stop justifying to others why it didn't work and start facing the harsh reality of why you gave up.

Stop justifying your excuses. The real problem with justifying your excuses is that the more you internalize your excuses, the more your mind starts believing that they are true. They get embedded in your mind as actual truths and facts. You train your mind to think that your excuses are justified and okay. This is a dangerous cycle and place to be. How do you get out of this place? Simple. Whatever goal you set for yourself, start by saying, "I control my success and take complete ownership of why I failed. I failed because of the choices and decisions I made. If I want to succeed, it's on me." You need to free yourself of all the garbage you have been feeding yourself, and the only way to do that is by taking ownership.

Settling is another excuse we often embrace. Settling is living a life of mediocrity. Don't ever settle if something doesn't work out at first. You need to keep going. Failures will happen and are part of life. Successful people are willing to fail more than anyone else. Remember, every failure is a life lesson and how you choose to respond is the difference. Do not accept your life for where it is, but rather lead your life to where you want to go. You may need to be your own hero at times. It will be lonely, and that's okay. People will not be there for you all the time, cheering you on. More times than not, you will need to find the discipline to continue. Remember why you started.

That tension you feel right now is where the growth will happen in your life. Don't use the resistance you face as a reason to start making excuses, but rather embrace it

SUCCESSFUL PEOPLE ARE WILLING TO FAIL MORE THAN ANYONE ELSE.

as a time of growth. Get out of your comfort zone and understand that staying there will never take you to the next level. Get comfortable being uncomfortable and never settle.

You only get one shot at this thing called life. There is no warm-up. There is no practice. You only have today. So stop making the excuses for why you didn't achieve something and instead begin doing something great. Maybe you need to start over, or you can pick up where you left off. It doesn't matter. What matters is that you press forward.

> **GET COMFORTABLE BEING UNCOMFORTABLE.**

Don't take your dreams to the graveyard with you because of your excuses. The Leveled Up Life and excuses don't align. It will never work. Remember, God's gift to us is potential, and our gift back is what we do with it.

CHAPTER 7

MINDSET IS EVERYTHING

"If you ready to take your game to the next level, you gotta change that mindset."
Eric Thomas

How you think and how you feel every day is unequivocally going to impact how you live your life. Most people wake up and just go through the motions of life. The average person, upon awakening in the morning, immediately turns to their phone to read e-mails, look at their social media notifications, and respond to any other pop-ups or banners they see first thing. This is often followed by turning on the television to watch the news and read an online newspaper. After getting ready and while heading into work, the same people will often listen to some more news during their commute. This is not the way to live and build success. Does this sound like you? If so, don't worry, I was once there too.

YOU ATTRACT WHAT YOU TRANSMIT

What most of us don't realize is how this negatively impacts our day. Just like our physical body, our brain is a muscle too. Every single thing we see, hear, or read will impact how we feel and how we go about living our day. Our emotions affect our actions. Our actions determine the life we are going to live. When we feed our brain with positive energy, it produces more positive energy in how we feel and think. When we feed our brain negative energy, it creates more thoughts of fear, anger, or hate.

There is a philosophy in life that says you attract who you are. Put out negativity to the world and you will attract more of it. Put out good and positive energy into the world, and you will attract more of that. We'd much rather be on the latter side.

Let's start with the news. What do you see? What do you hear? It's always about some tragedy involving death, trauma, injury, or hate. You rarely hear about all the good and success in this world – and there is a lot. The media knows what grabs people's attention and, unfortunately for us, it's the trauma and gossip of the world. As humans, whenever we hear or see something tragic, we can't help but want to hear about what happened. Why does the media continue to focus on all the negatives? Because it sells. Here's the problem. It doesn't serve you for the better. But for them, creating sensationalism is good for business because people get pulled into it.

The news will affect your mood. When you see a horrific story or something tragic happen, you begin to live in fear. You start asking yourself whether this could happen to your family or you. Reading a political social media post may anger you because you disagree with it.

Your mood is wholly affected by what you consume. And if everything you take in has an adverse influence, it is not a healthy way to live when trying to improve your life for the better. Mindset is everything, and when you go through the motions of life, such as watching the news, it will negatively impact how you live your life and the level of success you can achieve. I like to call this "living life by default." You accept life for what it is rather than leading your life to where you want to go. You don't guard your mind against the energy that won't serve you. Living a life by design is when you lead your life for where you want to go. You are intentional about what you read, whom you surround yourself with, and what you allow into your life.

> LIVING LIFE BY DEFAULT – YOU ACCEPT LIFE FOR WHAT IT IS RATHER THAN LEADING YOUR LIFE TO WHERE YOU WANT TO GO.

Your mind is a very powerful tool. What you consume controls your thoughts. Your thoughts influence both your actions and your beliefs. Your actions then determine the life you are going to live. Remember, you are a product of the choices and decisions you've made up to this point. But it all starts with how you think.

CHANGING HOW YOU THINK

The primary way that you're going to be able to change your mindset is by being very intentional about your choices and decisions each day. For example, if you wake up and are intentional about only reading or listening to topics that serve you for the better, you will benefit from living a more positive life. The books that I read and the motivational videos I watched completely impacted my life for the positive for years. This still holds true today. It affected my overall attitude, my stress levels, and so many other areas in my life for the better.

You will start to see life through a different lens. When you are intentional with what you consume, you train your mind to seek out more goodness in the world without realizing it. Here is an example. Ever buy a new car or like a car in a specific color and then, as you drive around town, you begin seeing that same car everywhere? Exactly. That's because your brain subconsciously starts focusing on finding that car. It's not that there are more of those vehicles all of a sudden. It's how your mind begins to think and operate. It's the same with your mindset.

When you intentionally focus on the positive in the world, you will start to see things differently and handle your life differently throughout the day. Is having the discipline to intentionally consume only positive material each day going to be easy? Absolutely not! But if you want to better your life to reach your goals and improve your overall well-being, you will need to be intentional each and every day about what enters your mind. It doesn't need to be perfect, but it needs to be something you focus on daily.

A PERSONAL TURNING POINT

I remember building my business early on and suddenly I hit a plateau. The business wasn't growing. I wasn't quite sure if the business could grow anymore. I was struggling. I started looking around for the next secret or some quick fix for success. I began waiting for someone to tell me what to do or save me. I felt it was some simple thing that needed to change. This went on for almost two years before I struck a pivotal point in my life and business.

I was in Disney World for a business trip that I'd earned for my earlier success. I was leaving a nighttime party with my wife and saw another fellow in the business who was far more successful than me. The room was dark, and he was far away, but I got the courage to walk up and approach him as everyone was walking out. The conversation was short but powerful. I told him my situation in about two sentences. My business plateaued, and it wasn't growing. He immediately responded and asked what my personal development plan was. Was I growing myself as a person? Was I reading personal development books on leadership, mindset, facing adversity, handling obstacles, growing a business, etc.? I wasn't. When I told him, he said, "That's the problem. *You* need to grow if you want your life and business to grow."

That was an eye-opening conversation and made me face a harsh reality. I'd heard about how important being on a personal development journey was, but I ignored it. I didn't need that. I was a successful New York State Trooper, a father, a husband, and someone building a business. I didn't need any rah-rah incentives to motivate me to work.

I always worked hard. The problem was that I didn't have the skill set to grow myself or my business any further than it already developed. I had to learn new skills, think differently and act differently if I wanted things to change.

Jim Rohn, entrepreneur, author, and motivational speaker, once said, "If you want more, you need to become more." This was precisely my problem. Rohn further added, "You need to work harder on yourself than you do on your job." This was all eye-opening to me. I needed to stop trying to work harder and learn how to work smarter. I needed to commit to my personal growth as a human being for that to happen.

I took the advice of my mentor at that party and immediately committed to a personal growth journey. Once I started doing this, I remember thinking, "This is the greatest secret on earth! Why doesn't everyone do this?" The way I thought, the skills I learned, and how I thought all began to shift.

My advice to you right now is do not do what I did. Don't think that committing to your own journey of personal growth is not for you, that it is not something you need. The person you are right now will not get you to what you want to achieve tomorrow. The world doesn't need to change. You don't need a big break. In the end, you need to be the one to change. It's 100 percent on you. Reading a book like this gives you a tremendous head start because you are already committing to growing yourself. But you cannot stop growing after one book. This is an endless journey that needs to become part of your daily routine. Commit to yourself now. Be willing to change for the better and commit to growing yourself.

DEVELOPING A PERSONAL GROWTH JOURNEY

When I finally decided to commit to this personal growth journey, I began reading and listening to a good personal development book for at least ten minutes a day. Since this was a new habit, I knew I had to be intentional about it. If I simply woke up and hoped I found time in the day to read, it didn't happen. I needed to schedule the time to do this.

My favorite author when I started was John C. Maxwell. I read his new book at the time, *The 15 Invaluable Laws of Growth* (2012). It is still one of my favorites today, and I have read it multiple times. It was blindsiding to learn of all the areas in my life that needed improvement. I even began looking at myself differently, in a more positive way.

I recommend ten minutes a day because you still have to go about your everyday life. You will still have to handle all that life throws at you – work problems, family problems, sickness, death in your family, etc. Sticking to this new daily habit will help you overcome life's challenges, and you will even find that how you respond to life's obstacles begins to change. Your attitude will start to improve. If you can give more than ten minutes a day, fantastic! Go for it. Don't stop. But you can't read or listen for only two or four days a week. It has to be done daily for this to truly work. It has to become a habit like brushing your teeth. I know some of you may be thinking, "I don't have time for this. I'm just so busy. I have a full-time job. I have multiple kids. I barely have enough time to eat!" Let me share with you how I managed it.

I employed something that I like to call your "hidden minutes." It's all the time throughout the day when you can do two things at once. For example, the time spent showering, brushing your teeth, doing your hair, or getting dressed. Or the time you spend commuting to work or running errands. Or the time you spend folding laundry, vacuuming your house, cleaning the dishes, etc. This is all time that you could also be doing something else, such as listening to a personal development book at the same time. With smartphones today, you have an encyclopedia of knowledge at your fingertips.

I frequently buy audio books from the Audible app and listen to them throughout the day. I turned my car into a mobile university, so I now listen to a good book instead of listening to the news or music. I do this even when my kids are in the car sometimes! If I can help my kids' mindsets start thinking positively at such a young age, why not? When cleaning up after dinner, I often have my headphones on listening to my book or some other motivational message I can find on YouTube. The point is that we all have our hidden minutes each day, and if you are intentional with them, you will find a lot more than ten minutes a day to commit to your personal development journey. It's incredible how quickly you start feeling better about life and how better you feel overall.

> START FINDING AND USING YOUR HIDDEN MINUTES TODAY TO IMPROVE YOUR LIFE. WE ALL HAVE THEM.

Start finding and using your hidden minutes today to improve your life. We all have them.

Besides the books that you read, there's something else I need to talk to you about. It's your environment. It's the people you surround yourself with every single day. You've likely heard it said that you are the average of the five people you spend the most time with. That is a powerful fact that holds true today. Here lies the problem. The average person wakes up each day and merely goes through the flow of life. Whatever happens, happens. They accept what they listen to, read, or see to control how they live. Your environment is unquestionably going to impact how you live every day.

If there are people in your life who aren't serving your mindset positively through something as simple as their social media posts, you need to limit your time with that person. They will drain your energy, and you only get a certain amount of energy each day. The same goes for people who are always causing drama in your life. You need to limit your time with them too. Some of you may be thinking a lot of drama takes place right in my own family. I'm not telling you to cut ties off with your family or best friend, but you may need to limit how much time you spend with them if they are draining you each day.

We all need to focus on having engines in our life. These are people who lift us up, not bring us down. Anchors in our life are people who bring us down. Stay away from them. When you commit to a personal growth journey, surround yourself with people who will lift you up, people who are more successful than you. Remember, you will never be criticized negatively by someone more successful than you. Surround yourself with those people. You may be saying to yourself, "David, how am I going to do this? No one around me is trying to commit to a high level of success like I am." That's okay. Your mentors early on will come from the books you read or the videos you watch. If you commit to them, you will start to see doors opening for you that bring you closer to like-minded people. It can be something as simple as becoming a part of an online group from a book that you read. Or it can be the people you follow online, such as me. The point is to be intentional and both surround yourself with and follow more successful people than you.

Nothing happens overnight, but I promise that if you commit to a personal growth journey today that includes reading or listening to a personal development book at least ten minutes a day, the way you think and live your life will be in a different place thirty days from now. Remember, if you want things to change, the only thing that needs to change is you. Life will never get easier. You need to get better.

> **IF YOU WANT THINGS TO CHANGE, THE ONLY THING THAT NEEDS TO CHANGE IS YOU. LIFE WILL NEVER GET EASIER. YOU NEED TO GET BETTER.**

Your morning routine will dictate how the rest of your day will go. How you live your first hour in the morning often determines how the other twenty-three hours of your day will go. I have a very structured morning routine that I live by. I'm a big believer that when you take care of yourself first, both physically and mentally, it's going to impact those closest to you positively. The habits I formed early in the morning don't cost me time. They buy me time back. I have more energy throughout the day. I am more confident. I am less stressed, and I can impact the world in a better way. Additionally, those most important to me, such as my family, will benefit when I am acting and feeling in a positive light.

My morning routine starts the night before. You may ask, "How does your morning routine start the night before?" Let me explain. I set my phone to "Do Not Disturb" at 9:30 the night before. This way, I don't receive text messages or phone calls throughout the night. There is nothing worse than being sound asleep and hearing the ding of a text message at two in the morning. You need your sleep for so many health benefits, and good sleep carries over to how you are the following day. No interruptions throughout the night are crucial. You may be saying, "What happens if there's an emergency? How will anyone get in touch with me?" Most phones today have settings that allow certain people's phone calls to ring, even on Do Not Disturb. My family members are all marked as "Favorites" on my iPhone, which enables this feature. It won't allow their text messages to go through, but phone calls will ring. If it's an emergency, the person will call, not text me. My Do Not Disturb goes on at 9:30 every night until 6:00 the next morning.

I also shut off all notifications on my phone, including all pop-up banners on my locked screen and the little number in the corner of an app that tells you how many notifications you have. I shut all these notifications off because when I get up in the morning, it's "me" time. It's time to set myself up for success and a productive day. It's easy to wake up and get sucked into endless notifications, e-mails, and alerts. Most people wake up in the morning, and immediately grab their phone and dive right into their in-box, their social media, or any other notifications or banners on their phone. This is detrimental to your daily success and both a time and energy sucker. You need to prime yourself for the day. That stuff can wait. It will be there in an hour. When the first hour of the morning is solely focused on you, you will be a better version of yourself for everybody else.

For me, my alarm goes off at 4:30 in the morning. I get up, put my workout clothes on (often laid out already from the night before), walk downstairs, drink my pre-workout drink, and immediately do ten minutes of meditation. You may be saying, "I can never meditate. My mind never stops racing." I thought the same thing, but about two years ago I was at a place in my life where I constantly felt my mind was doing a thousand things from the second I woke up to the second I went to bed. I was feeling overwhelmed with life and burned out, so I had the courage to ask for help. I connected with a therapist, and she immediately said, "David, you need to start meditating before all of this gets even worse. It will help calm your mind and give you a sense of peace." I was willing to try because what I was doing wasn't working. I needed to make some profound changes before I had a nervous breakdown.

Most people assume meditation is weird behavior or some deep form of praying. It's not. It's really about sitting down in a quiet place and focusing on nothing but your breathing. Many meditation apps are pretty simple to follow. It's often guided by someone who walks you through the meditation. You can choose to have light music playing in the background or the sounds of nature, such as waves crashing on the beach, making it even more relaxing.

But something started happening throughout my day, which was pretty impactful on my life. The breathing exercises performed throughout meditation focus on slowing your breathing. This is done through long inhales and exhales. It is a natural way to calm your mind and body. When you are agitated or feel overwhelmed, your body responds with quicker and shorter breaths. Your senses are also heightened, playing into your stress. Here's the powerful part. When faced with an aggravating life issue, you will begin to consciously slow down your breathing rate. It will help you remain calm. When this started happening to me, I was honestly blown away. A simple ten-minute exercise I did each morning led to my mental well-being throughout my day. That's the power that comes from taking ten minutes of your day to work on a practice like meditation.

After meditation, I exercise from thirty to sixty minutes a day, six days a week. Here's the truth. You know exercise is good for you physically, but it's also just as good for you mentally. All the endorphins, or feel-good feelings, the brain releases during exercise will carry over throughout your day. Many will say, "But David, I don't have time to exercise." I say it doesn't cost you time. It buys you time back. How? You will be more efficient throughout the day, get more done in the same amount of time, and be less stressed. Don't use the time excuse for why you can't take care of your health and exercise. Everyone is busy. You have the time.

I perform this morning routine before my kids get up because once they're awake, it's game on. I truly believe in the power of having a morning routine, so it sets you up for success throughout the day. Ever take a flight somewhere, and when going over emergency procedures, they say, "In case of an emergency, put the overhead oxygen mask on yourself first before helping others?" They say this because you cannot take care of someone else efficiently if you can't care for yourself.

Too often, people burning the candle at both ends are completely stressed out and exhausted. We need to change that, and having a solid morning routine where we put ourselves first can be that change. It's not being selfish by any means. It is selfless because it will positively help others.

One last point I need to share. You need to guard your mind like a prison. The way you think and feel are going to affect how you live your life every day – I 100 percent guarantee it. Living a life by design will require you to be intentional about doing many of the things I shared above. It's not going to come easy and will require you to have the discipline to change your current habits. But it will be worth it. The person you are right now will not get you to the goals you want to achieve tomorrow. You're going to have to go through a growth journey, and it's going to start with the way you think and operate in your life. We all have our hidden minutes, and I fully believe you can make those changes starting today.

> THE PERSON YOU ARE RIGHT NOW WILL NOT GET YOU TO THE GOALS YOU WANT TO ACHIEVE TOMORROW.

The Leveled Up Life was never meant to be easy, but it's a way of living. It's a way of life. Change the way you think, and you will change how you live your life. Mindset is everything.

CHAPTER 8

YOU MUST BE WILLING TO MAKE SACRIFICES

"If you don't sacrifice for what you want, what you want becomes the sacrifice."

Unknown

I f you have goals, if you have dreams, if you have things that you want to accomplish in life, the harsh reality is that you cannot achieve any of it if you continue to do the same thing every single day. Today, most people are waiting for their life to become easier, less busy, or more convenient. Most people are waiting for their life circumstances to ease up on them. They wait around month after month, year after year, for their life to be perfect. Maybe it's fewer after-school activities for their kids? Perhaps it's working fewer hours at work? Perhaps it's until they have some extra money in their bank account? Maybe it's until they have spare time in their life? Perhaps it's until their family supports them?

The truth is nothing in your life will change for the better if you aren't willing to change what you are doing and willing to make sacrifices. You won't wake up one morning with extra money in your bank account or spare time on the clock. That doesn't exist. If you are not where you want to be in life, it has everything to do with you not being willing to make the sacrifices and nothing to do with what life hands you each day. As mentioned before, there are people in this world who are in worse situations than you who are highly successful. They never allowed themselves to fall into the victim mentality trap and instead found a way to make sacrifices in their life for the better. If you continue to do the same thing every day and hope that things get better for you, you will be waiting for the rest of your life. It's never too late to alter the choices and decisions you make so you can improve your life. What happened until now is in the past. It comes down to what you are willing to do today to improve your life tomorrow.

DON'T SACRIFICE THESE INGREDIENTS FOR SUCCESS

It's not about waiting for the perfect moment, the ideal time, or the consummate opportunity to finally go after your goals and dreams. That perfect moment in time is never going to happen. It's about creating it. It's about understanding that once we take 100-percent owner-ship of our lives and are willing to make the necessary sacrifices, things get better. It is a very freeing moment in life when we take full ownership. Why? Because when we rely on something other than ourselves to succeed, we give someone or something power over us. That never works in your favor.

When you give this power to others, you will subconsciously procrastinate your success, waiting for someone else to do it for you. It is a complete sense of freedom when you take ownership. You no longer rely on others. It will become a pivotal moment in your life. You will go from living the victim mentality to victor mentality and start seeing significant progress in your life.

> THERE IS NO WARM-UP IN LIFE; THERE IS NO PRACTICE LIFE.

People often live their lives going through the motions, hoping things get better. Remember, there is no warm-up in life. There is no practice life. You only have today. What you do makes a difference today. The choices you make today do matter. How you act and the decisions you make count.

I sense by this point you are starting to see how I live my life and how certain principles I am sharing with you come up in multiple chapters. This isn't happening by accident. I'm sharing it from multiple angles because it has to become part of your everyday life. We often need to hear things more than once in order for them to stick.

I remember seeing Gary Vaynerchuk speak at an event a few years back, and he shared a powerful story. When he was in his early twenties, he spent much time with ninety-year-olds. He would often ask them to tell him about their lives. "What is your story?" Every time he asked them this question, it started with the same two words. "I wish." They'd say, "I wish I'd done this" or "I wish I'd taken that opportunity." They'd lived their life with regret. The struggle will always be less painful than regret. You don't want to become part of that story. Make the sacrifices and changes today to live the life you want to live tomorrow. It won't be easy, but it's the price everyone must be willing to pay to succeed.

Once I had built my business, I often talked to people who struggled with getting started on their journey of success. I tried to mentor them but often hit a roadblock that I couldn't figure out. They had big dreams and goals, but when the time came to put in the work to make the necessary changes and sacrifices, most of them did very little or nothing at all. Finally, I started asking more questions and dug a little deeper. I realized many of them were waiting for permission to start. They waited for others to say it was okay to pursue their dream. Often they looked for this go-ahead from those closest to them, such as their mom, their dad, or even their spouse.

Remember this. The only person who needs to give you permission to do anything in your life is the one you see in the mirror every single day. That person is you. It is nobody else's job to support your goal or your dreams but you. It was placed in your imagination from God, the Universe, or whomever you believe in. It is for you, not for them. If you want something to happen, you need to make it happen. It's on you as an individual to rise and grind and put in the work. This is your life. These are your goals. Don't ever wait for permission or someone else to support you before you decide to start. Take that first step. Believe in yourself. Everyone has to be willing to take that first step. Even you. Like I said earlier, struggle is less painful than regret. You can do this. This is a Leveled Up Life.

Doing the same thing repeatedly and expecting different results is the definition of insanity. You cannot continue doing the same things today as yesterday and expect to reach your goals. Additionally, the person you are now will have to experience a growth journey to achieve your goals tomorrow. In short, you need to become more and change for the better. There are 86,400 seconds in a day, and what you do with your time each day will determine your success. Do the same thing, and you will get the same results. Change what you are doing in a productive way, and your life will change for the better with it.

> TODAY, WE MAY HAVE TO DO WHAT WE DON'T WANT TO DO TO LIVE THE LIFE WE WANT TO LIVE TOMORROW.

In life, we must understand that today we may have to do what we don't want to do to live the life we want to live tomorrow. It will look a little different for everyone, but the underlying feelings of being uncomfortable or putting in extra work are the same. We all must be willing to pay the price.

So how do I change, you may ask? What is it that I need to do? Here are a few suggestions. First, success leaves clues. Find someone who has what you want and do what they do. Study them, observe them, read their books. But remember, you must be 100 percent coachable and teachable for this to work. What do I mean by this? You don't know it all. If you did, you would be successful in that area of your life. You must be willing to learn and listen more than you talk. I've heard we have two ears and one mouth for a reason. So, we must listen more and talk less. If you are fortunate enough to know this person personally, ask them if they would give you thirty minutes of their time so you can ask questions. Offer to take them to lunch. Yes, it may cost you a few dollars, but it can pay you back tenfold later. If you don't know anyone personally, that's okay too, and that's how it was for me. I then relied on reading their books or watching their videos online. There is always a way to find someone successful in whatever you are trying to pursue and study them.

SACRIFICES FOR SUCCESS

Over ten years ago, when I started this journey of making sacrifices and personal growth to improve my life, I quickly realized how much I needed to change. I never had a plan for the day. I would wake up and just go about my day. Whatever happened, I dealt with it as it came, and I was never intentional about how I managed my time.

My days often started by getting up in just enough time to get myself and the kids ready for the day. My wife left earlier than me, so I was responsible for getting my kids ready and off to daycare. I remember getting to work in my suit (I was a State Police Investigator, aka Detective, so we wore suits) often in a full sweat. I would sit down at my desk for about ten minutes, waiting for my body to cool down after the morning rush was over. That was one of the first things I needed to change. How?

I needed to start getting up a little earlier to allow myself more time. Yes, it would require me to sacrifice some sleep, but clearly what I was doing at that time wasn't working or a healthy way to live. I was stressed all the time and felt a sense of burnout from the constant rush. At the same time, I also knew I needed to get healthier. My wife and I decided to get up an hour earlier (before our kids got up) to exercise at home, as you know. By the time we were done, we felt a thousand times better mentally and physically. My wife would get ready for work feeling less stressed, and I would get our kids ready in a much better mental state. Yes, there were still days I would show up to work in a full sweat, but how I handled myself and how I felt was completely different. Giving up sleep was quite a sacrifice, but it made such an impactful change in our life.

After work, I came home, watched some television, ate dinner, played in some men's softball leagues a few nights a week, watched some more television, got my kids ready for bed, and hit the sack. It was the same process over and over. This was layered with habits that weren't serving me for the better. I felt like I was just flowing through life. I was going through the motions. I talked about being intentional with what you do in your life. I was doing the exact opposite.

So, what if I eliminated watching television every night and instead read a personal development book? What if I cut back on how much softball I played and instead worked on growing additional income with my part-time business? What if I watched some motivational videos online before bed to inspire me to get up earlier the next day? Would any of these changes make a difference? You bet they did. Together, they made a drastic difference!

I decided to fuel my mind with something positive rather than watch mindless television. I also decided to use the time I spent playing softball to build a business instead so I could create more income for my family and get out of debt. Now don't get me wrong, I wasn't always in work and hustle mode. I still played some softball, but I cut it back considerably. As for watching television, I will admit that I eliminated that at night. When my family or co-workers were all together, they would often talk about a particular television show as a topic of conversation. When they would look at my wife and me, we would just chuckle and say we don't watch television anymore. They would look at us quite perplexed, but we were on a mission to radically improve our lives, and watching television wasn't moving us closer to our goals. As I said, you need to make sacrifices in your life, and, for us, it meant giving up a little sleep and eliminating any activities we did that weren't serving us. We were on our path to the Leveled Up Life.

You need to ask yourself what you are doing right now that you could cut back. Do you watch a lot of television? How much scrolling of social media do you do each day? Want to shock yourself? Go into your smartphone settings and review your screen time usage. You will be surprised by how much time you spend doing mindless things. Now imagine what would happen if instead you used that time to do something that improved your life, such as building a business, exercising, reading a book, etc. Successful people don't have more time, but they know how to use their time wisely. They manage their time more effectively.

In life, we need to give up to go up. You need to be willing to give up what you are currently doing if you want to go up in life. Or, better yet, we need to give up the good to go for the great! No one is immune to the craziness of life. We will always be swamped and pulled in a thousand different directions. However, once we learn to change how we respond, make sacrifices, and change what we are doing, our life will begin to change.

COMMON SENSE ISN'T ALWAYS COMMON PRACTICE.

This isn't some big secret I just shared with you. Everyone knows if they make some changes like exercising and watching less television, it will help them. But common sense isn't always common practice. It must be top of mind each day. You must be intentional with the changes you want to make and reflect on them at the end of each day. Ask yourself this one simple question: "What could I have done better today?" Then immediately the next day, improve on what you learned from the day before. Be willing to be better than you were yesterday. Build on that each day, and you will quickly find out how much more you get done. How much more efficient you are and how your mindset and the way you see and handle your life improves for the better.

Nothing is ever going to be easy the first time. You may fall. You may blunder. Some days you may slip back into your old ways. If that happens, that's okay. Give yourself that grace. You are human. Each day is a new day, and you control your choices and decisions each and every day. Don't beat yourself up. Make the necessary adjustments and press forward the next day. Give up those things that aren't serving you and replace them with something that will. Every successful person must make sacrifices. You may not see them, but they do.

As I write the end of this Chapter, I can tell you that I needed to get up even earlier than usual because of all the things I needed to get done today. You don't see this, but I will tell you it happened. It was a sacrifice I made. We all must be willing to make them if we want to succeed at the highest levels in life, the Leveled Up Life.

CHAPTER 9

FACING YOUR NAYSAYERS

"You will never be criticized by someone who is doing more than you. You will only be criticized by someone doing less."

Unknown

I want to start this Chapter by telling you that the vast majority of people in this world live an average life. They work a regular nine-to-five job Monday through Friday and look forward to the weekend to relax, have time off, do what they want to do. They accept their life for what it is rather than lead their lives to where they want to go.

I want to be upfront in speaking about this. If someone is 100 percent content with where they are in their life when it comes to their career, finances, relationships, level of self-fulfillment, and everything else related to the current state of their life, then kudos to them. I am happy as long as they are happy. Maybe that is you. If so, then great! You are happy with where you are and therefore I am utterly happy for you. However, living a Leveled Up Life speaks to the other group of people who are not content with where they are and want more out of life. My guess is those of you reading this book want more out of life.

Ninety-eight percent of society today lives what I call "a life by default." I spoke about this in Chapter 7. They live the life described above and are okay with it. But what about the remaining 2 percent? What type of life do they live? I say this group of people are living "a life by design." They live life on their terms. They don't allow anyone or anything to stop them from creating the life they want. Besides not allowing their life circumstances to stop them, they certainly understand they cannot let other people's opinions of them prevent them from living this 2 percent life.

GOING AGAINST THE NORM

If you want to live a 2 percent lifestyle, this life by design, you must understand that you will have to pay the price along the way. When you go against the norm of what most people do, you will be criticized for your choices. However, remember this. People's opinions of you have nothing to do with you, but everything about how they perceive their own lives. Maybe trying to build a side business while also working full time and being a busy parent seems utterly unrealistic to them. So, when they see someone else doing it, rather than openly supporting them, they criticize them, telling them it won't work.

I remember the criticism I received during my early years building my home-based business while still working full time with the State Police. My business was a network marketing company that I truly believed in. I had a vision and took the

> **PEOPLE'S OPINIONS OF YOU HAVE NOTHING TO DO WITH YOU, BUT EVERYTHING ABOUT HOW THEY PERCEIVE THEIR OWN LIVES.**

time to educate myself on how the compensation plan worked. I honestly trusted in what it could do for my life and understood exactly how it worked. However, I was ridiculed both openly and behind my back for what I was doing. People would say things such as, "It's a pyramid scheme," or "What a waste of time," or "It's a scam." People laughed at me. People mocked me. But I learned that they weren't laughing at me for actually pursuing a side business, but instead were criticizing me for their perception or experience with something like this. Just because they didn't have the same vision or understand the compensation plan as I did, didn't mean I should quit or give up. That was their perception. Not mine.

Sometimes criticism will be hurtful and amplify that fear we already possess. It may stop us dead in our tracks and, too often, prevents us from pursuing our goals and dreams. This is a harsh reality you must be willing to face and understand. However, if you know this up front, you will be prepared later on when it starts to happen, because it will happen. No one pursues something against the norm without receiving some reproach. It is all part of the process.

It is a very natural instinct as human beings to disparage others for what they are doing. Unfortunately, with the world we live in today, social media makes it easier for people to criticize others. It is very easy when sitting behind a keyboard to say something harsh or cruel. Most won't say it to your face but have no issue publishing a negative comment on your post, which crushes you internally. Think about it. Have you ever put up a social media post and received a handful of positive and uplifting comments, but then one person says something negative? Instead of focusing on all the positive comments, you get caught up on the single negative one. Our brains are wired to protect us, and that's why we respond that way, but it's our job to recognize what is happening and move on. Their opinion doesn't define you.

If you want to live an extraordinary life then you need to be willing to do remarkable things. Dealing with naysayers or haters is one of them, and it's not meant to be easy. I've dealt with them myself and I'm still dealing with them today, even as I write this book. You just need to keep reminding yourself that this is part of the process. People will say harsh things, but you need to develop a stronger mindset to move on. I often use the phrase "bless and release," meaning thank you for the comment, but it's time I let you and the comment go. Bye-bye. I simply move on. The more negative comments you get, the better you will be at dealing with them. As

> EMBRACE THE NEGATIVITY AS A SIGN YOU ARE GOING SOMEWHERE THAT MOST AREN'T WILLING TO VENTURE.

a matter of fact, if you aren't getting any negative comments, then you probably aren't stretching yourself enough! Embrace the negativity as a sign you are going somewhere that most aren't willing to venture.

CRITICISM FROM UNLIKELY SOURCES

Here is something I need to impart that I feel is very important to know about the people who will criticize you. More times than not, the harshest critics will be your family and closest friends. I remember my niece's birthday party a few years back. I was standing in the family room of my sister's house, and my wife and I were talking about retiring early from our full-time careers because of our business growth. We were having a drink, and, between a sip of beer, my brother, who I love more than the world, kind of chuckled at me. I don't remember his exact words, but he said something about our plan and the goal as unrealistic. It hurt and stung, but I understood where he was coming from. We were trying to build a business, to achieve a goal, which most people fail to do in life. We were trying to create a career and path for our life that was very unconventional. However, that was his perception. It wasn't wrong what he said, but it wasn't our perception. We had the vision, and we had the drive to do it. You don't need someone else's support or permission to do something. All that matters is that you believe in what you are doing.

A quote I live by is, "Other people's opinions are not your reality." I highly recommend you write that down somewhere, store it in your phone, and repeat it until it is

OTHER PEOPLE'S OPINIONS ARE NOT YOUR REALITY.

memorized. Your life and your reality are what you make of it. Not what someone else says it should be. I see many people living a life based on how others feel they should live it. This leads to a very unsatisfied and unfulfilled life. You cannot change who you are. Your goals. Your dreams. Your likes and dislikes. They are yours and in your imagination for a reason.

I remember the phone call I made to my mom from my basement apartment to tell her I wanted to pursue a career as a police officer. I was in my early years of college, and my parents were divorced at the time. My father worked for the police department, and I knew what I was about to tell her wasn't going to go over well. I was right. My mother wasn't happy. She didn't want me to do it. She may have even cried. But in my heart, I knew it was something I had to pursue. It was my desire. My goal. My dream.

Far too often, people pursue a particular career path based on others' opinions of what they should do. Every parent would love for their child to grow up to be a successful surgeon, dentist, or lawyer, but if it's not for you, you shouldn't pursue it. You need to follow your heart and your intuition, not someone else's. Steve Harvey, comedian, actor, and host of *Family Feud*, once said, "Your goals and dreams were placed inside your brain by God for you." They weren't meant for someone else.

You will never ever be critiqued by someone more successful than you. I know you have heard this already – it's that important. It just doesn't happen. You will also never be criticized by someone who has already achieved what you are trying to accomplish. People who are highly successful or have already achieved their goals truly understand what it takes to get there. But your loudest and harshest detractors will come from those who never actually walked in your path. I haven't had one successful keynote speaker tell me I shouldn't speak. I never had anyone who built a similar business tell me it wouldn't work. I never had another author tell me that writing a book is impossible. However, I have endured an endless number of people who never accomplished anything tell me what I was doing was a waste of time. What is my best tip

PROVE THEM WRONG.

on how to handle these types of people? Prove them wrong. Go out there and do the work and prove them wrong.

At the end of the day, the only person who needs to believe in whatever you are trying to accomplish, as mentioned earlier, is the person you see in the mirror every day. That person is you. If it's in your heart and you have a pulling towards it, then that's all that matters. You don't need anybody else's permission to go after your goals or dreams. Not your mother's. Not your father's. Not your best friends' or your siblings'. You just need yourself. That's it. Other people don't define you. You define yourself.

THE SNOOZE BUTTON

Using the snooze button for your advantage is a great tip I have. Let's get back to social media for a second because I believe more hate and criticism comes out on social media than anywhere else because of the ease for people to do it. I often had to restrict or "snooze" certain people I was connected to on social media. Their constant negative comments on my posts or their rants on social media were mentally exhausting for me. It may not rise to the level where you need to block them or disconnect from them online completely, but hitting the snooze button on someone is okay, and I encourage you to do it too.

When you hit snooze, you won't see their constant negative drama-driven posts or deal with their sarcastic comments. It is freeing to have this power. If you have people like that right now who aren't serving your mindset for the better, hit the snooze button. Don't feel bad about it either. Every single human being on this earth has their own problems in life. No one is exempt from them. But maybe right now, while you are trying to improve your life, constantly seeing your close friend complain about something over and over frustrates you. You spoke to them about it. You wanted to help them. But nothing changes. If that's the case, hit the snooze button.

I sometimes even hit the snooze button on people I agree with. Here is an example of why. During the 2020 Presidential Election Campaign, political posts on social media were running rampant. No matter what side of the House you were on, you could easily get caught up in the drama and become frustrated throughout your day. So even people I often agreed with, I snoozed. Why? Because those types of posts created a thread of arguments and disagreements that would only frustrate me further. Similarly, this could hold true on your view of masks for children during the pandemic. Whether you agree or disagree, the same scenario applies. Every single day I guard my brain like a prison. I only let in what I feel will serve my mindset for the better. I'm not perfect, and I don't try to bury my head in the sand to the world around me, but I do protect it. The snooze button is a powerful tool of relief. Learn to use it sometimes.

When I started growing my business early on and surrounded myself with people who were also trying to improve and grow their lives, little did I know the impact it would have on my mindset. I felt motivated. I felt driven. I felt positive. I started seeing all the good in the world rather than the bad. Who you spend your time with will significantly impact where you go in life. If you spend most of your time with people who whine and complain, who are dissatisfied with their career, then you too will find yourself whining and complaining all the time and be dissatisfied with your career. They say your income is an average of the five people you spend the most time with. If you take the time to think about that, you will realize it is probably true. You want to put yourself in a growth environment. In an environment with people who are going places in their lives.

Now you may say, "But David, I don't know anyone like that." My response to you is that's okay. Neither did I at first, but I found them through the books I read, or the podcasts I listened to, or the YouTube videos I watched. It's just like you reading this book, even though you may not know me. I realize that I've written this earlier and you may have heard me talk about these points, but they are important to repeat and carry over to all the lessons I am sharing with you. Sometimes we need to hear things a few times before it sinks in. Authors of books from afar may become your growth environment and mentors. You want the people you interact with most to become your life's engines – the ones that fuel you and lift you up, not the anchors of your life who will bring you down.

> YOU WANT THE PEOPLE YOU INTERACT WITH MOST TO BECOME YOUR LIFE'S ENGINES – THE ONES THAT FUEL YOU AND LIFT YOU UP.

I want to close this Chapter with this last point about the naysayers. It is often our harshest critics who eventually come around and compliment us on what we achieved. The number of people I worked with on the State Police who gave me such a hard time who have come back amazed at what I accomplished is astonishing. I was at a State Police golf outing one summer day waiting in the dinner line, and one of my fellow Troopers said, "Dave, honestly, I can't believe what you have done and created for yourself. I should have listened to you back in the day and joined you. It's awesome to see. Congrats." I couldn't believe what I was hearing because this person was one of the harshest detractors early on. But here's the thing. I didn't stop or quit because of what he used to say.

You cannot quit or give up because of the hurtful things people say, which create massive amounts of fear. You need to see past this and know when you succeed, they will come back around and tell you in due time. Most will; some won't. For those who won't, it's not because they didn't see you succeed. It's because they are probably too embarrassed to admit they were wrong.

CHAPTER 10

CONSISTENCY

"It's not what we do once in a while that shapes our lives, it's what we do consistently."
Tony Robbins

Y ou wake up one early morning, begin scrolling social media, and see one perfect picture after the next. You see a picture of someone in great physical shape who has three kids and wonder how they did that so quickly, or you see someone in the same business field as you crushing their goals in what appeared to happen overnight. It's all a bit much to handle, and you immediately begin comparing yourself to those people. I will talk about comparison in the next Chapter because it is something we all face, but I want to talk about something else here – consistency.

What you see on social media is often the highlight reel of someone's life. For the most part, people aren't willing to show their struggles to get there. People aren't willing to show what they do behind closed doors, when no one is watching, that brought them to today. The truth is there is no such thing as overnight success. Ask someone successful about their journey, and you will soon find out how disciplined they were and how often they failed. People aren't willing to openly share all the hard work it took to get there, and it does an injustice to the many people who start because the perception is that it happened overnight. Well, I am here to tell you it didn't.

> **WHAT YOU SEE ON SOCIAL MEDIA IS OFTEN THE HIGHLIGHT REEL OF SOMEONE'S LIFE.**

It took months and months and more likely many years for someone to get to where they are today.

You may come across the occasional person who hit the lotto or the mom and dad who passed them a fortune to live with, but that is not the norm. Don't get it twisted in your mind. The vast majority of successful people were very good at one thing – being consistent day in and day out, even when they didn't feel like it.

THERE ARE NO OVERNIGHT SUCCESSES

I just finished an hour-long keynote presentation on resilience, and I was standing at the back of the ballroom. I usually like to stick around for a few minutes after speaking to connect with people after I conclude my speech. I often hear about a struggle someone has that they want to improve on, or sometimes it's just to say hello and a simple thank you. After this event, a gentleman came up to me and said, "That was beyond inspiring and powerful.

The way you shared everything was so compelling. Did you take classes on speaking or any sort of training?" My answer was, "No. I didn't." He was kind of taken back as if he didn't believe me.

I could tell by his reaction, so I explained. "I spoke to groups of people in a small library ten years ago. You should have seen me in the beginning. It was nothing like this. But after years of practice and being consistent, I got better each time I did it. This consistency over ten years brought me to where I am today and to groups as big as 20,000 people at the Superdome in New Orleans." Of course, that doesn't include the hundreds of videos I completed on YouTube, Facebook Live, and Instagram, which also provided regular practice throughout those ten-plus years."

The same holds true with my network marketing business. People would join our team and see where I was at that moment and get frustrated after just a few months if they didn't have the same success I was experiencing. I regularly explained to them that my current success represented years in the making. The person you see today is not the same person I was when I first started. It took years of consistency, hard work, and growing as a person compounded over time to lead to my success.

Our company sets a benchmark they would like reached every month, a barometer of whether we are moving our business forward. It involves a certain level of productivity that, if attained, indicates we are on our way to building a solid business. When I mentor new people on our team, sometimes it comes up that I've hit that benchmark over 120 months in a row. That is ten years of continually moving my business forward! I share this so people understand I didn't create a million-dollar business overnight. I did it by being consistent for years. Tiny little incremental steps steadily compounded over time led to success.

I strongly agree that we live in a microwave mentality, and it gets worse by the day. Need the definition of a specific word? Easy. Google it. You have the answer in half a second. Need to order something online through Amazon? Great, it will be here in two days. This wasn't how I grew up. I remember as a child that if you collected a certain number of UPCs (barcodes) from cereal boxes and mailed them to the company, they would send you a prize or small toy. Here was the catch. After you collected ten UPCs and mailed them in, processing, shipping, and handling would take four-to-six weeks. Four-to-six weeks! You heard that right! Imagine that?! I recall going to the mailbox every day, starting around the three-week mark (hoping they would be early!), checking for my prize. But more times than not, it would take every bit of the six weeks. That is not the case today.

With today's technology, anything you could ever want or need is at your fingertips. Here is the problem. This does not represent reality when it comes to success. You can't get six-pack abs overnight. You can't build a million-dollar business overnight. You can't become the expert in a subject in under a week. This perception often leads to early frustration and the reason people often quit. But suppose you are willing to separate yourself from this new reality of instantaneous gratification and understand that building long-term success will take patience and unwavering dedication? In that case, you will win in the end. Otherwise, you will be set up for disappointment and frustration. You need to let go of achieving significant results in a minimal amount of time. You need to trust the process of consistency.

Let's say you started a brand-new workout program and finished your first session. You feel great, take a shower, but you look exactly the same when you look in the mirror. You do the same thing the next day, and you still look the same. Why? Or let's say you put a ton of work into your new business for an entire week, and when you look at your bank account after that first week, you made nothing. Why? Both of these scenarios are similar and very discouraging. Why? Because you put in the hard work and see nothing in return. However, what you need to understand is how consistency works.

The definition from the *Oxford English Dictionary* says it is "acting or doing in the same way over time." The key here is "over time." Success comes from repeatedly taking daily actions that, compounded over time, lead to massive results. You keep working out every single day, and after a few weeks, you drop a few pounds. Or you work your business consistently every day for a month and finally earn a little more income. You don't realize that those small daily behaviors that you commit to are moving the needle. You may not feel like you can see any improvement, but progress is happening. You need to be patient and understand the process.

MOMENTUM

You know what kills more goals and dreams every day? The starting and stopping cycle so many of us practice. I see it all the time. People are highly motivated to build their business, get fit, or go after some scary goal, and they come roaring out of the gate at full speed. "I'm all in! I'm going to crush it!" This goes on for about two-to-three weeks, and then life happens. Someone gets sick. They got stuck at work. Their kids' activities take up all their time. So they stop. Then a few weeks go by, and the same thing happens again. They get motivated and are "all in" for a period of time, and then they stop again. Honestly, it kills me to see this happen. Why? Because when they finally create some consistency and suddenly stop, it kills momentum.

The more times they start and stop will, eventually, lead to permanently stopping. Why? Because no one can tolerate the frustration they must deal with by constantly starting over. It just doesn't work. So, consistency can work against you too, in cases like this. If you are continually starting and stopping over time, the compounded frustration will eventually cause you to quit.

In his book *The Compound Effect* (2010), Darren Hardy talks about pumping a water well. At first, trying to pump the water out of a well manually takes much effort. You pump, using a lot of muscle and energy to get the water to start flowing out of the well. But once the water starts running, you can almost ease up and it will still keep flowing. You were consistent, and momentum kicked in.

However, if you stop pumping, in just a matter of seconds the water will stop, and you will lose all that momentum you created. Here is the problem. When you start again, you have to repeat that entire process. All that effort. All that momentum you built was lost. It's exhausting. Ask yourself right now. How often have you started and stopped something? I'm sure you can name quite a few times. It's okay if you did, but what you need to understand going forward is that this can't continue if you want to achieve your goals. You must start, be consistent, and stick with your plan no matter what.

TO BE CONSISTENT, YOU WILL HAVE TO WEATHER THE STORM OF LIFE.

I need to address something that I feel is super important. To be consistent, you will have to weather the storm of life. You will have to find a way to push through and remain constant during the tough times of life. Life happens to all of us. We all face our trials and tribulations, and life has a funny way of throwing curveballs at us right at the moment we say we will commit to something. During these times, we need to remain consistent and avoid the start and stop cycle.

A few years back, my wife and I were with my mother-in-law and our kids at the school carnival. It was a beautiful spring evening in May in New York. Our kids ran from one ride to the next, having an absolute blast with their friends. My mother-in-law mentioned that she found a lump in her breast that needed to be checked out. This caught us by surprise, as it would for anyone. Little did we know there was an aggressive cancer raging inside my mother-in-law. In under four months, she passed away. This was a devastating loss for our family. My mother-in-law was healthy otherwise, with no signs that this was coming. No one saw it coming. It all happened very fast.

My wife and I could have stopped pursuing our goals and dreams of building our business. I could have easily quit making videos or speaking to people at events. But we never paused. We never gave up. Why? Because we understood the importance of consistency. We understood that if we stopped then with all the momentum we had created, it would be next to impossible to start over again and get back to where we were. My point here is to be prepared and understand that you need to be consistent to be successful. You must find a way to show up even when it's hard. You may be asking, but how? How do I remain steadfast? I am going to get to that right now.

WHAT IS YOUR "WHY"

You cannot achieve anything significant without having a "why" attached to it. Why do you do what you do? What drives you? What will keep you going during those tough times? What motivates you to get up in the morning and keep showing up? What makes you stay awake into the late hours of the night working when you could be in bed? It all comes down to your why. Your why is what drives you. But let me elaborate on this.

It has to be bigger than you. It can't just be about you. Having goals personal to you is fine, but there will come a point in your life when you will hit something a lot tougher than you. This event often causes people to quit.

You need to have a driving force for why you do what you do, and it has to be bigger than yourself. It might be your kids, spouse, or family member.

I read a story about a mother whose child got stuck under a car being repaired after it collapsed on the child. If the vehicle hadn't been lifted off the child immediately, the consequences would have been deadly. The mother single-handedly lifted the car and was able to free her child. I'm sure any other time, it would have been impossible for her to lift up a car, but not when her why was attached to her child's life. Her why was so much bigger than herself. Her child was facing possible death, and she did something that otherwise would seem impossible.

Your mind and body will amaze you when it's attached to something bigger than you. It will push you to remain consistent during the hard times. I encourage you to anchor yourself on your why each day. Use your why as your anchor, the thing that keeps you laser-focused and grounded to push yourself during those tough times. If you can learn to have a strong why, staying consistent will be much easier for your life. Ask yourself right now. What is your why?

One of the hardest parts of being consistent is feeling motivated to start. I used to think I needed to wait until I felt inspired before I started, but actually, it was the other way around. You need to start, and eventually you will feel motivated. Why? Because motivation doesn't hit us like a bolt of lightning. Yes, you can watch an inspiring

> ANCHOR YOURSELF ON YOUR WHY EACH DAY. USE YOUR WHY AS YOUR ANCHOR.

video that will pump you up for a few minutes, but you will need the discipline to begin when the time comes to take action. A lot of the time you won't have motivation when you first set out. This is where focus and control come in. You cannot be consistent if you don't have the discipline to do the work. What drives discipline? Your why. Everything works in synergy. Your why drives discipline, and discipline leads to motivation. Ultimately, as you start being consistent, you will begin to feel the motivation kick in, which compounds over time the longer you stick with it.

I remember that first day my wife and I committed to changing our lifestyle to become healthier and more fit. Getting out of bed at five in the morning seemed next to impossible. We started in the winter months, so not only was it cold getting up, but it was also dark outside. Our motivation on a scale of one-to-ten was a whopping zero. But we forced ourselves up and did it. How? Our why drove our discipline. Once we were done and showered and dressed for the day, we felt a huge sense of accomplishment. We felt motivated. We felt excited about what day two would bring. Day two came, and again it was a struggle. But we remembered the feeling we had once we were done. Right there, that little bit of motivation kicked in at that moment. We got up and did it again. Two days led to three. Three days led to a week, and it continued.

We were able to remain consistent every day. At first, the drive and inspiration weren't there, but the more we did it, the more motivated we felt. The more motivated we felt, the more consistent we became. Days turned into weeks, and weeks turned into years, and now we both live a healthy lifestyle today. We remained consistent even when we didn't feel like it early on. So, to the common excuse I often hear, "I don't feel like it," my answer is, "Who does?" Who likes getting up early in the cold? No one. But we must be willing to have the discipline to create the consistency needed for success.

As you remain consistent, understand it's not always going to look pretty. Many days you will feel exhausted just showing up, and the results will be average at best. That's okay. The important part of consistency is that you *show up!* No. Matter. What. The days that make it count are the days you don't feel like showing up. Unfortunately, I hate to tell you, but there will be batches of time where every day seems like a struggle. Give yourself the grace and understanding that you are human and that your feelings matter. It ebbs and flows like anything else in life. However, this is not an excuse to stop. This is not an excuse to give up. This is not an excuse to say it's not working. It's a reason to press forward and do the work to remain consistent. Like I said above, the small incremental steps compounded over time lead to success. These hard days are extremely important to reach your end goal. So brush yourself off, get back in the saddle, and keep going.

> THE DAYS THAT MAKE IT COUNT ARE THE DAYS YOU DON'T FEEL LIKE SHOWING UP.

Last but not least, take it one day at a time. Don't worry about how you will drop those one hundred pounds or build that six-figure business. Understand that this is all part of the process of living the Leveled Up Life. It takes effort, and it takes work. I remember when I began speaking in a small library, and I thought about the potential of one day becoming a paid speaker. I didn't know how it would happen or even how to get there. But what I did know was to focus on being my best that day.

Remember to live by this principle, yesterday is in the past. Tomorrow is not guaranteed. All we have is today, so that's all you need to worry about at this very moment. Show up and be disciplined today, and the rest will take care of itself. One day at a time. One step at a time. This all leads to consistency, and your consistency will lead to your success.

CHAPTER 11

COMPARISON

"Comparison is the thief of joy."
Theodore Roosevelt

I honestly believe that it is a more challenging time right now, than ever before, for people not to get caught up in the comparison game. Social media is at our fingertips, and we spend hours each week, sometimes hours each day, scrolling through our favorite social media platform. We compare our looks to someone else's. We compare our success to someone else's success.We compare our family to another family. We compare our relationship to someone else's. The comparison trap can quickly unfold every day because, unfortunately, these scenarios are presented to us on our phones every waking moment.

This poses a huge problem. We find ourselves never content with where we are. We never give ourselves credit for what we have already accomplished. We will never be happy. It will create fear. It will amplify doubt.

Why? Because we are constantly comparing ourselves to someone else in all areas of our lives.

During the early days of growing my business, I regularly saw other people who seemed just like me, hitting some big lofty goals. As much as I knew I could do it too, it also put me in a mindset where I felt I was lacking. Rather than looking at my own life and how far I had come in all areas of life, I instead focused on what I didn't have based on what I saw.

I even struggle today. When I decided to pursue being a keynote motivational speaker, I couldn't help but compare myself to other very successful speakers. I, too, got caught up in the comparison game. These were people I looked up to, was inspired by, watched daily, and listened to everything they did. They say find someone who has what you want and do what they do. I agree with that, but as long as you can stay focused on where you are and not compare yourself to the person you are following. When I catch myself going down the comparison trap, I remind myself of the same things I want to share with you here.

YOU VERSUS YOU

First, and I think maybe most important, don't compare your chapter one to someone else's chapter twelve. We are so quick to compare ourselves to someone who has already been doing it a lot longer than us. We are on day one, yet we get frustrated with our lack of success after seeing someone who has already "made" it. You cannot do this! Every day is a competition against yourself. It's you versus you. It's not you versus the other person and where they are. That doesn't serve you for the better.

You are on your journey, and your focus must be to compare you to you only. Where were you yesterday compared to today? Are you better today than you were yesterday? What did you learn yesterday that you can improve on today? What didn't you do yesterday that you can do today to move forward? Strive each day to be a better version of yourself rather than striving to be like someone else who started years before you. This is *your* story. This is *your* journey in life. We are all different individuals for a reason, and our own timeline starts at a unique season. Focus on yourself and your timetable, not someone else's. No two stories of life are precisely the same.

What you see others post or share is what we often refer to as their "highlight reel." We touched on this trend in the previous Chapter with regard to consistency, but it is very meaningful in our discussion on comparison. Most people are not willing to share the ugly, the struggle, or the hard work it took to get there. Everyone wants to post their fancy car, house, or extravagant vacation, but very few are willing to be open and honest about what it took to get there – the struggle they may have had along the way, the lack of support, the haters who criticized them, all the failures they had along the way. People are afraid to be vulnerable and share the things that paint the whole picture. (As a side note, don't believe everything you see. I have seen people post a photo as if they own that "fancy car" or "fancy house" and find out it's not even theirs!)

In this comparison trap, we often compare our everyday life to the highlight reel of someone else. Think about that for a second. We scroll social media and see this facade of others and, without even thinking twice, we compare this to our everyday life. No one lives on cloud nine their whole life. That is not normal. That is not reality. If people were willing to share the struggle and be vulnerable, it would better serve everyone and minimize this highlight reel comparison trap we often fall into.

Remember, no one on this earth goes through life without their own trials and tribulations. Even the people we see online who make it appear as if everything is all sunshine and rainbows have failed more than we know. Human beings struggle. We all struggle. It's part of who we are as a society. I will be the first to tell you that writing this book has been one thousand times harder than I could have ever imagined. What I thought I could do in a month is taking ten times longer. When I first started, I would often ask, "Who am I to write this book?" I have struggles too. But if you see me post about being an author, don't get caught up comparing yourself to me. It has been a long, upward battle. Everyone must pay the price for success. There are no free passes.

I like the Theodore Roosevelt quote at the beginning of this Chapter, so I think it bears repeating, "Comparison is the thief of joy." It creates the domino effect of all the negative emotions that can quickly derail us or hinder us from ever starting. Instead of counting our blessings, we get caught up in a mental battle of what someone else accomplished. This causes us to feel down about ourselves or lowers our self-esteem. It generates negative self-talk. It casts fear and doubts with our own goals and dreams. I understand it is tough not to compare ourselves to other people, but if we are willing to take a step back, recognize it for what it is, and hinder its progress before it spirals out of control, we will be well on our way to eradicating this mental trap.

PUTTING THE PAUSE ON THOSE WHO INSPIRE YOU

You may disagree with this point, but it is similar to something I shared earlier regarding our nay-sayers. In Chapter 9 we discussed that it is perfectly fine to press the snooze button on your detractors and naysayers. But it is also true that when you are growing and trying to hit a big goal or achieve success, you may need to limit your interactions with those who already did it. Why? Because sometimes, the best thing you can do while trying to stay focused is not put yourself in a position where you even begin to compare yourself to someone else. Whether you snooze someone on social media for a bit or limit your messages with this person, it's all up to you.

If you genuinely struggle with being able to compartmentalize your journey and not compare it to others, the best advice I can give you is to limit your ability to see them during that timeframe. You are not holding anything personal against that person (more times than not, it's someone you look up to), but seeing their life is not serving you.

There is a very successful entrepreneur I look up to who represented exactly this for me. It was hard to pause him because I truly love this person and all they have accomplished. He inspired me. He motivated me. He let me know it was possible! But at times, I caught myself comparing. I was trying to get my business off the ground, and seeing him hit benchmark after benchmark wasn't helping my mojo. So, without hesitation, I paused his posts and stories on social media, so they were no longer at the top of my homepage. I admit I wasn't perfect. I watched his stories every few days because I often learned a lot from this person, but I had to limit how often I did it. It was nothing personal. It just wasn't serving *me*. Don't hesitate to do the same if needed. They will never know.

> YOUR SUCCESS IS DEFINED AS WHERE YOU ARE TODAY COMPARED TO WHERE YOU FIRST STARTED.

Remember, that your success is defined as where you are today compared to where you first started. It is not defined from where you are now compared to where someone else currently is. Read that twice. Twice. Furthermore, if you constantly compare yourself to someone else's success, you will always be disappointed because there will always be someone who is further ahead of you in life no matter how successful you are. Someone will always be doing more than you. You can be a millionaire, and there will still be someone else who is further along. Be okay with that. It's normal. I can't stress enough that you are on your own journey. This is your life. You can acknowledge where others are but never define your success compared to someone else.

GRATITUDE

Last but not least, have gratitude for where you are and all you have. To date, for every single problem you have ever encountered, you have a 100-percent success rate. How do I know that? Because you are still here. You survived. You lived. So instead of comparing yourself to someone else, compare yourself to how far you have already come.

Sometimes you need to sit down and remind yourself of all you have accomplished. Find a quiet space and think of all the things you have done with your life to this point. Maybe you got that degree. Perhaps you purchased that home. Perhaps you lost that weight once before. Maybe you completed that 5K race. Perhaps you have children and are raising them to be good human beings. Maybe you paid off some debt. Perhaps you helped someone in a time of need. Perhaps you volunteered somewhere and impacted someone who has less than you. Maybe you just picked yourself up once before when you struggled. It doesn't matter what it is.

We have all accomplished something in our lives. We all have things we can be grateful for that we can use to remind ourselves of how far we have come. Comparing ourselves to others serves no purpose. So stop doing it and start believing in yourself and where you are going.

In summary, I want to leave you with this thought. You have no room for comparison in your life. That's not what the Leveled Up Life is about. We don't have time to waste and we especially don't have time to waste on something that doesn't serve us. Learn how to recognize the comparison phenomenon when it happens, remember what I shared with you above, and change the course of your thinking as quickly as you catch yourself falling into this trap. It's okay if it happens, but it's not okay to allow yourself to stay in this negative mindset for long. You must make the necessary adjustments so it doesn't continue. If you need to "call an audible," then do it and snooze the person causing you to compare. It's time to start focusing on you and rid yourself of the comparison garbage that isn't serving you.

CHAPTER 12

DON'T EVER QUIT

"Struggle is less painful than regret."
Unknown

Throughout my life, whether it's been saving for that batting cage, becoming an ocean lifeguard, making it through the State Police Academy, building my business, becoming a keynote motivational speaker, being a parent, being a husband, or any other chapter of my life, it has always been a thousand times harder than I ever expected. Nothing I ever achieved in life has been easy. It has always been a lot more work than I anticipated, and I have failed a lot. I often remind myself whenever I set out to achieve a new goal that I need to prepare myself for how much more difficult it will be mentally than I imagined. With that being said, if there is one principle I have lived by my entire life, it's don't ever quit. No matter how hard the challenge is, quitting can never become an option.

I have mentored and helped hundreds of people both in my career with the State Police as well as building my business. Every one of the people I have helped along the way has always started off motivated with big goals and great intentions. Whether studying for that promotional exam to attain the next rank or trying to get on a particular detail, such as the K9 Unit of the State Police, or building a six-figure business from home part time, they all verbally expressed their commitment to doing it. More times than not, "life" happened, aka they got busy, excuses crept in, motivation was lost, the blame game started, and they gave up. They quit on themselves and had a thousand excuses for why it didn't work, and unfortunately, 99 percent of the time, it had nothing to do with themselves, but instead, they passed the blame onto someone or something.

AT THE END OF THE DAY, THE ONLY PERSON YOU ARE CHEATING IS YOURSELF.

At the end of the day, the only person you are cheating is yourself. The only person you truly let down is that person you see in the mirror every day. That person is you. The people around you don't care that you quit, but we feel the need to make excuses to others to make ourselves feel better.

On a different note, I felt bad for the people who gave up because I saw their potential. Once they shared it with me, I saw the vision of their life if they didn't stop or give up. I often believed in people more than they believed in themselves. Why? Because I knew it was possible. As a regular guy, if I could do it, so could they. I knew how much better it felt, pushing through all the challenges and still making it happen. I would help them envision the life they could create if they were willing to never give up. I challenged them to Level Up their Life. Some heard me but also listened. But more times than not, most heard me but never actually listened. What do I mean by that?

Many heard what I had to say, but it went in one ear and out the other. They never actually took what I said to heart and went after it. They quit, they gave up, and they didn't actually listen. Those who didn't quit or give up went about their lives much differently. They went about it a lot like me. They did listen. That is what I would like to talk to you about in this Chapter. Never quit, no matter what.

PERSEVERANCE & SUCCESS GO HAND IN HAND

My favorite word in the dictionary is "perseverance." It's the name of my team in business, it's my corporation's name, and it's a word I live by every day of my life. I have an iron scripted sign with the word "perseverance" hanging in my office just above my head, so I see it every day. The *Oxford English Dictionary* defines it as "persistence in doing something despite difficulty or delay in achieving success." I live by this word because it reminds me daily of what it will take to succeed. It lets you know that difficulty is part of the process. It reminds me that the timeframe I want to achieve something is often not the same time it truly takes to get there.

You cannot succeed at anything if you don't have perseverance. You cannot win at anything if you don't have perseverance. Perseverance and success come hand in hand. You cannot succeed without perseverance. So maybe it's time you print this word out and hang it by your bathroom mirror or have it as your screensaver on your phone or even read the definition to yourself every day. No matter what you decide, you need to remind yourself that at the root of all success is being willing to persevere to achieve your goal.

When you quit or give up, you are settling for less. You are resigning yourself to mediocrity. Instead of leading yourself to where you want to go, you give up and accept your life for what it is. This is often followed by blaming others or playing the victim card. This is not a winner's mentality and never works out in the end.

When I speak to an audience, I often share that "God's gift to us is potential, and our gift back is what we do with it." We all have potential. Yes, that means you too! We are meant to live a life of excellence, but we are selling ourselves short when we give up.

STRUGGLE VERSUS REGRET

This leads to my next point. Struggle is less painful than regret. You've heard this already, too. When I started sharing my story and speaking to people on a smaller scale, I realized I had a natural ability to inspire and motivate people. I started feeling an internal tug to pursue the path of being a paid keynote motivational speaker. As it always does, doubt crept in. How do I get my name out there? How will I even start? Who do I reach out to? Who will listen to me? I am not good enough to speak at that level. Similar doubts and self-talk surfaced when I built my business online. Who will support me? Who will trust me? Who will buy from me? I don't have a big following, so this won't work. The list goes on and on, but I reminded myself that the struggle of making this happen was far less than the regret I would experience if I didn't try. I don't ever want to look back at my life and regret that I didn't do something out of fear and the price I wasn't willing to pay to get there.

I remember the time I was sitting in the nose-bleed section of a large audience of a few thousand people for the annual conference of my business. It was recognition time. I watched a handful of people walk across the stage receiving accolades for their significant accomplishments as people cheered. I was happy for them, but at that very moment, I didn't cheer. I sat there in silence, staring at that stage with a poker face. What was going through my brain was much different from what was going through the people's minds cheering to the left and right of me. I was saying to myself, "Why not me? If they can do it, so can I."

I knew it would be hard work to achieve such success, but after seeing others do it, who appeared to be no different from me, I knew I would regret it if I didn't try. In that instant, my inner fire was lit, and my motivational drive kicked into another level. I remember my wife turning to me, asking, "What's the difference between you and them?"

I said, "Time. They just have time on me. That's it. If they can do it, so can I." A new vision was born at that very moment, and I wasn't going to allow the work it would take to get there stop me. You need to understand that regret is mentally painful. You can't turn back time. It's over at that point. So pursue your goals and use your time wisely.

> YOU NEED TO UNDERSTAND THAT REGRET IS MENTALLY PAINFUL. YOU CAN'T TURN BACK TIME.

FAILURE VERSUS QUITTING

The truth is that nothing good comes from quitting. We never hear an inspiring story that involved quitting. We never hear about a successful athlete quitting during their journey to get there. We never hear about a successful entrepreneur who quit. We will often hear about all the failures they experienced, but they never gave up.

Quitting produces nothing of value. It's doesn't serve your life for the better and doesn't help those around you either. Those who succeed understand this. No matter how hard it gets, they never stop. They may make adjustments but they never quit. Quitting is permanent and guarantees one thing – failure. So please, don't make yourself believe that giving up is a better course of action because it's not. You don't grow and will undoubtedly fail when you quit. Did Michael Jordan ever stop? How about Michael Phelps? Or Kobe Bryant? Or Serena Williams? None of them ever quit.

If you are reading this book, you woke up today with a new day. You have another 86,400 seconds to do something great with it. I see this as a sign that God isn't through with you yet. If he were, you wouldn't be here today. Each day you wake up is an opportunity to go after your goals. You have complete control of the choices and decisions you make today. Remind yourself that this day could be a great day if you are willing to work for it and make no excuses. Seize the moment each day. Seize this opportunity. Use your hours wisely. Do not let the day get away from you, doing mindless things that don't move you closer to your goals. Understand what's in front of you, and it's time to get out there and make it happen. You have the time. Use it wisely.

As you go through life, remember that failure is part of the process. Those who are successful fail all the time. They are willing to fail more than most people and never give up. Remember my lifeguard story and how I failed the still water test multiple times? Or the batting cage story and the challenges I faced?

Before writing this Chapter, I just received an e-mail from someone telling me they selected someone else as the keynote speaker for their annual convention. This is after I had a great phone call with them that I thought went really well. I felt certain I was going to get the spot. But I didn't. It hurt. It created doubt. But I won't stop.

By continuing to move forward, you grow stronger mentally, and your mindset focuses more on the positive. I fail every single day of my life. If I am not failing, I am not trying. Failure is always knocking on my door, whether it's from a challenging workout that pushed me or just being turned down for business. I have learned to accept it for what it is, not dwell on it, and move forward. Don't let failure derail you. It happens to all of us. Failure doesn't define you. Your true character is developed by what you do with your life when failure occurs. Don't ever quit;

instead develop the character of a true winner who never gives up.

You always must be willing to make adjustments along the way. Whatever plan you initially had will always have to be tweaked as you move forward in your blueprint. You create a road map of what it will take to hit a certain level in your business or what you need to do to achieve a specific goal, and then a thousand things come up that you never expected. What do most people do? They play the victim card and say, "It wasn't meant to be." That's a lie. It's not that it wasn't meant to be. It's that you must be willing to pay the price. It's all part of the process. It's what happens when we pursue goals and dreams.

You need to adapt to the obstacles and overcome them. Don't make excuses. Make adjustments to your plan and move forward. Evaluate the problem at hand, see what course correction you need to take, and, without hesitation, take action. Better yet, take massive action and continue to move forward! The adjustment phase of success may happen a thousand times over, which should be expected.

> DON'T WORRY ABOUT HOW YOU WILL GET TO THE TOP, BUT RATHER HOW YOU WILL FACE THE PROBLEM IN FRONT OF YOU RIGHT NOW.

I firmly believe that 99 percent of not giving up is being aware of all the little life lessons, like the ones I am sharing with you in this book, and applying them to your life. They're almost like "life's secrets." Once you learn them and apply them, you are less likely to give up. Why? You recognize the issue at hand, you course correct, make adjustments, and you move forward. It's that simple. Block out all the noise and continue to put one foot in front of the other. Don't worry about how you will get to the top, but rather how you will face the problem in front of you right now.

DON'T PLAY THE BLAME GAME

This is one of my favorite points regarding quitting and never giving up. Do not blame others for your lack of success or play the victim card. It is no one else's job to support your goals and dreams but you. No one in my life handed me anything. Every single thing I ever achieved I had to work for. I often see people give up and blame others for their lack of success. "This person didn't do what they were supposed to do," or "That person didn't do what they said they were going to do." If we were truly willing to hold ourselves accountable as much as we try to hold others responsible, the world would be a better place. You instead need to ask yourself, "What did I not do? Where did I fail?"

Last night my wife and I called a family meeting around the center island in our kitchen to talk to our three daughters about taking ownership and not blaming others for their lack of success. Recently, we started hearing more excuses for why they didn't get a good grade on a test, didn't do well with a sports game, or didn't have time to study. I don't blame them for saying this because it's a human instinct to blame something other than ourselves. But I wanted to point out to them that in life, they need to take total ownership of their lives and where they are.

When you blame others, you give someone else power over you. When you are willing to take ownership of your life, it's freeing. The same goes for playing the victim card. Life is not out to get you. We all face our own trials and tribulations. We all have our demons we must face. No one on this earth avoids tough times, but those living a Leveled Up Life live with a "victor mentality" rather than "victim mentality."

I remember during the early days of building my business, I waited for other people to free me of all the obstacles I was facing. I waited for people to free me by supporting me rather than criticizing me. I was waiting for people to free me of all the "no"s I was getting and, instead, give me a "yes." Finally I realized that it had nothing to do with anyone else but had everything to do with me. I needed to free myself. You don't know when your last day on earth may be, and if you constantly play the victim card you may be held hostage by yourself for the rest of your life. Losing my best friend made me realize I could not wait around for others to rescue me. It was my job to rescue and save myself. I am not the victim. I am simply someone who is growing and, along the way, I will face hard times. It's that simple.

As you know my wife and I give ourselves twenty-four hours when something tough happens to us. We get twenty-four hours to complain about what happened, but then it's time to get over it and move on. We don't quit. We don't blame. We don't play the victim. We brush ourselves off and keep on going. This is something we try to instill in our kids. That's how we left off with our daughters last night. I told them, "When you're grown up, and

Mom and I aren't here one day, you need to remember that you can live a very successful and fulfilling life. But you cannot blame others or play the victim card for your lack of success. It is on you. Own it and move on."

QUITTING AFFECTS OTHERS, TOO

This leads to my next point. When we quit or give up, it doesn't affect only us. It affects everyone around us, especially those closest to us. People watch everything we do, but not what we say. As a result, many people talk about what they will do, but few actually do it. The problem is that people, such as our kids, take notice, internalize it, and apply it to their own lives. Our kids see it all – the mom or dad who announced that they were going to exercise daily but within a few days gave up or the business that a mom or dad launched, but closed down when it got hard. They know that Mom or Dad gave up. "If my mom and dad gave up, I guess I can too." That's not something I want to instill in my kids.

My wife and I have, for years now, shared life lessons with our three daughters. We play motivating messages in the car or listen to audio books that help us grow. We often get a roll of the eyes from them, or they ask us to change the channel, but we keep it playing anyway. Sometimes we sit them down, like we did last night, and talk to them about a life lesson we want to share. But as the years went by, as much as they hated it, we started noticing small but powerful things happening.

For instance, my wife and I were walking down the hallway in the upstairs of our home where our bedrooms are. We heard our older daughter, Cassidy, talking to our younger daughter, Addison, in her room. The door was mostly closed so we stopped to listen. We were able to make out that Addison was suffering from some self-doubt with how she looked and afraid of what her friends may think of her at school. Cassidy responded by telling her how lovely she was and how we are all unique and beautiful in our own way. Cassidy went on to tell her not to worry about what other people think of you. To be confident. To love yourself. I don't remember the other exact words, but my wife and I stood there with our mouths wide open in awe hearing this conversation. It was a proud Mom and Dad moment. Addison then rebounded and started living the way Cassidy told her to and we now see such a happy and vibrant kid developing.

Another example is the YouTube videos our daughter Sadie started making on motivation that she calls "Sadie says..." and then she follows up with a life tip. Little did we realize how powerful our actions had become and how they will affect the generations behind us.

The point is that every decision and choice we make and how we handle life's tough times will affect not only ourselves but also those around us. It doesn't just stop with our kids. It will also impact the people we work with and those we interact with daily. Don't ever underestimate the power you can have on someone when they see that you didn't give up. Your momentum of pressing forward creates more impact for those around you. I like to say the speed of the leader is the speed of the pack. When you don't give up and keep on going, you set the tone not only for your family but for everyone around you every day.

A few things to consider along your journey. Remember why you began and those feelings you had just before you started. The excitement. The motivation you felt. The vision of you achieving success. Use those emotions as your anchor to keep you going when it gets

DON'T EVER UNDERESTIMATE THE POWER YOU CAN HAVE ON SOMEONE WHEN THEY SEE THAT YOU DIDN'T GIVE UP.

hard. Those feelings you had when you first started always dissipate as you go through the process. It's almost impossible to stay super motivated and excited all the time. But if you are willing to anchor your why on those feelings, it will help you push through the tough times.

You have come far in life already, so don't forget those accomplishments as you pursue this new chapter in your life. Get a reward for what you have already done. Don't stop now. Don't give up now. It solves nothing. No one ever said it would be easy, but I am here to tell you it will be worth it. You were meant for great things. Now go out there and make it happen. Be willing to pay the price and never give up, no matter what.

PART THREE

THE PRINCIPLES AT THEIR CORE

CHAPTER 13

ALWAYS GIVE YOUR BEST

"God's gift to us is potential.
Our gift back is what you do with it."
Authorship Uncertain

As I begin writing this Chapter, I am sitting on an airplane at about 32,000 feet, heading to Salt Lake City, Utah. To the left and right of me, most people are watching movies, listening to music, having a conversation with others, or taking a nap. Please don't get me wrong. There is nothing wrong with any of these options, but right now, my priorities are in a different place.

I have a book to write that I want to get in the hands of all of you. The question is, how do I use my time right now? Use it leisurely and do one of the things the others are engaged in or make the best use of my time? You know my answer. Make the best use of my time and continue to write this book that I know can positively impact your life. I want to give you some background so you understand why this Chapter is significant to me and why I needed to write about it. We'll head back in time to my youth.

I joined the New York State Police as a New York State Trooper on November 2, 1998. In May, I graduated from the six-month, grueling Trooper academy and was stationed on Long Island for Field Training. I was then transferred to my permanent assignment in Peekskill, NY. By this point, in everything I did in my life, I always strived to do my best. To go after those lofty goals. To strive to do hard things and feel that sense of accomplishment. It was always about a sense of fulfillment and progress in my life, from saving for that pitching machine to being an ocean lifeguard and then as a New York State Trooper.

> IT WAS ALWAYS ABOUT A SENSE OF FULFILLMENT AND PROGRESS IN MY LIFE.

I always looked to be one of the best among the Troopers in the barracks. There was a handful of us who were very similar. They were also very hard-working, dedicated, and always tried to be their best. Each month we had a friendly competition. Who made the most DWI arrests in the month? Who made the most criminal arrests? Who led the station in activity for the month? Month after month, I was always one of the leaders and among the same group of Troopers. It wasn't because I needed to prove anything to anyone, it simply was the way I had always been. I always gave my best no matter what the circumstances. I didn't know how to live life any other way.

From the moment I realized that there was an award each year called "Trooper of the Year," I pursued that goal. It was a benchmark for me and something to go after. I worked hard at it every month, even when times were tough. It didn't happen overnight, and some of my closest friends and coworkers achieved this goal before I set my eyes on it. They worked very hard and deserved it. Eventually, through consistent hard work and always giving my best, in 2003, I was awarded Trooper of the Year. It meant a lot to me. I hit the benchmark I was striving for and continued in the life philosophy I had come to live by. *Always give your best.*

I was promoted in 2004 to Investigator, which was our detective level in the State Police, and they also had a similar award, called "Investigator of the Year." It was another benchmark to reach, and after a few years, I achieved that too.

As my career went on, I continued to pursue the next challenging benchmark, and, for me, that was the rank of Lieutenant. To attain this position, you had to take the most competitive exam in the State Police. If you did not place in the top twenty on the exam result's list, you most likely would not be reached to for a promotion. I studied months for this exam, every free moment I had. I studied at work when it was quiet or went to the library right after work. I would often finish the night at a local Barnes and Noble cafe because the library would close before I was done for the day. This went on for six months.

As well, I took two weeks of vacation time immediately before the exam to study more.

The day came for the test, and I finished up number seventeen in the State, which ultimately led to my promotion to Lieutenant in 2012. I was a Lieutenant in the State Police for five years, until I was promoted again (based on work performance) to Captain. I retired in 2021 with that rank. I finished my career running all State Police operations for the County of Westchester, NY. A highlight at the end of my career was serving as the Incident Commander for the 2020 US Open at Winged Foot Golf Club in Mamaroneck, NY. I was in charge of all police and emergency operations for this global event.

During my time with the State Police, I also began a direct sales business in 2010, known as multi-level marketing. I fell in love with the company, the people who led it, and what it did for my overall health and wellness. It didn't take long for me to set my sights on the top ranks and achievements in the company and go after them just as hard as I had with everything else. In only a few years, I reached the elite levels in the company and ultimately became a million-dollar earner in the business. Right now I am on this flight to Utah to meet with the CEO, the President, and a few other executives after being selected by them to be part of a board that represents the other 400,000 people in the company.

My success in business and my career with the State Police opened the keynote motivational speaking door for me, which I am very passionate about and am presently engaged in today. No matter what it is, the way I approach my life is the same – to always do my best.

I share all of this with you not to brag or give you my resume but to understand that good things will happen when you always give your best. Maybe not on your time-line (we'll talk about that in the next Chapter), but eventually, it will work out. No matter what I did, I strived to be better, to be the best version of myself. It didn't matter if I wasn't as good as someone else; what mattered was that I *did* my best to *be* my very best. That is what was most important – to live my life to my fullest potential.

My challenge for you is to honor anything that your name is on. Every single thing to which my name is attached, I give 100 percent. I give it my very best. I refuse to settle, and neither should you. Take pride in what you do. Don't just sign your name to something without giving it your all. Don't just flow through life each day, letting life dictate how you will handle your life. Remember, you control the choices and decisions every day, no matter what happens to you. Give it your best. Try harder. Understand there will be hard days and mistakes will happen, but this is not a reason to cut corners and not deliver your very best. I know some days will be taxing, and life will challenge you. But that's life, as harsh as this may sound. We all have our trials and tribulations. It's what you do about life that makes the difference.

Life doesn't reward average. Average is everywhere. It's what makes up the vast majority of this world. You never hear someone raving about an average restaurant or an average movie. Why? Because it's average. I once read that if all the money were taken away from everyone and

LIFE DOESN'T REWARD AVERAGE.

redistributed equally to everyone globally, it would end back in the same hands. Why? Because people who live a life of excellence get rewarded for it. You cannot perform at an average level and expect above-average results. Too many people want to win the trophy but aren't willing to do the work it takes to win the trophy. Too many people want to be a champion but aren't willing to do the work it takes to hold the title of being a champion. Their efforts don't match their expectations. You will need to be your own hero if you want to truly succeed. You will need to lead yourself to do above average. No one is going to do it for you. No one is going to hand you anything.

An Under Armour commercial portrays Michael Phelps and the hard work, grit, and dedication he delivered to achieve the level of success he did. He won twenty-eight Olympic medals in his career. Of those medals, twenty-three are gold, three are silver, and two are bronze. Simply outstanding! Phelps went above and beyond what anyone else has ever accomplished. The advertisement includes scenes of him swimming, eating, working out, and even vomiting during training because he pushed himself that hard. The commercial ended with two words – "Rule Yourself." If you want to succeed, you will need to be above average, way above average. Moreover, depending on how high you want to go, you will need to be your own hero to make it happen. More times than not, you will be solely by yourself. No one will be watching over you or pushing you to do more. It will be on you.

> **WHAT YOU DO IN THE DARK WILL BRING YOU OUT IN THE LIGHT.**

What you do in the dark will bring you out in the light. What do I mean by this? It's about all the work you do behind closed doors, that is, in the dark when no one is watching, that brings you out into public view, aka the light. For me, it was the thousands of hours working my business late at night on my computer or preparing my keynote presentations that no one saw. Or the thousands of times I got up at 4:30 a.m. to work out so that I could be the healthiest version of myself. No one was there to push me or motivate me. I was alone. Remember, ordinary people are only willing to work hard when someone is watching. Successful people always give their best no matter what.

We often take life for granted, but need to understand life is very short. My police career was over in a blink, and my kids are growing up quicker than I could have ever imagined. Remember, there is no warm-up in life. There is no practice in life. We only have today to make a difference and impact our lives. Far too often, we talk about *tomorrow* and what we will do when we are less busy, or it's more convenient. I know you remember that the problem with that thinking is that tomorrow is not guaranteed. We may not be here tomorrow. We only have today. What we do with each hour of the day matters much more than you think.

Successful people wake up each day delivering their best and don't worry about what they need to do a week or month from now. They focus on what they need to complete today and how they can give it their very best. We need to wake up each day with a sense of urgency and bring our very best no matter the task. This goes for what you do at work *and* how you handle yourself at home. What good is it if you are a public success and a private failure? What good is it if you have a very successful career but your family life is a mess? They both need to be in synergy to live our life to the fullest and live a Leveled Up Life. Always giving my very best means doing this both at work and home. I want to be the best business owner, the best speaker, the best father, and the best husband all at the same time. I can't be my very best in one area and not the other. Why? Because I truly believe that one side will affect the other. If you strive to be your very best, you cannot succeed in one area when you are failing in another. Maybe this is the sign you were looking for to finally change how you live your life each day, both publicly and at home. To be your very best, you must live this way in all areas of life.

IF YOU WERE LOOKING FOR A SIGN TO CHANGE YOUR LIFE, THIS MAY BE IT.

Next, have no regrets and understand you may not get a second chance. Often, opportunities will be presented when we aren't fully ready. That's just the way life is. This is often how life works, and if we don't seize the opportunities presented to us, we will live with regret later on. I often encourage others to lean into their fears. It won't be easy, but regretting something is far more challenging to deal with later on. Facing the fear and starting is less painful than regret, even when we don't feel ready. You will always have fear and never be ready. So, lean into it.

Remember why you started your success journey and understand that once you find your why you will always find your way. Why did you start? What drove you to go after your goals? Use that why as your anchor to start. Once you take your first few steps, the rest will take care of itself. You will always find your way.

Living a Leveled Up Life by always giving your best also means doing things when they are uncomfortable. Learn to live in the area of life where you always feel stretched, where it's uncomfortable. Get comfortable being uncomfortable. I constantly live in the zone of discomfort. Writing this book was challenging and uncomfortable. Being a speaker and presenting to hundreds or thousands of people can be uncomfortable. Building a million-dollar business was very difficult and uncomfortable. But that's what always giving your best requires. To live in the state of being uncomfortable.

I've heard that the number one source of fulfillment in life is progress. As humans, we must feel improvement in our life through accomplishments. It's fulfilling, rewarding, and keeps our minds motivated and at peace. How good does it feel when you hit a big goal? Or accomplish something you have been working on for a while? Or how do you feel after spending hours cleaning your house, and you are finally done? You feel great! You feel a sense of accomplishment! Why? It's progress in your life!

> **I AM ALWAYS STRIVING TO BECOME A BETTER VERSION OF MYSELF TODAY THAN I WAS YESTERDAY.**

I always set benchmarks in my life. I am always striving for purpose or object. This way, I feel like I am always making progress in some area of my life, and a sense of fulfillment always lives inside me. I am always striving to become a better version of myself today than I was yesterday. When I strive to be better than yesterday, it brings me closer to my goals and the benchmarks I set. Those who sit around and do nothing become stagnant and often feel depressed. Why? There's no progress in their life. We need to strive to move forward each day.

When you give your best, you never know the impact you can make on someone else. Often we don't even realize the impact we had on someone through a straightforward conversation or one small, almost meaningless, task. A simple smile to someone walking into the grocery store could change that person's mood for the better. Maybe they are dealing with a severe sickness or suffer from depression, your smile might give them hope. Perhaps it's holding the door open for someone who feels life is against them right now with all their current struggles, but your gesture helps them see life differently.

The point is that when we live each day with our shoulders hunched over and head held down, that attitude will carry over to the energy of other people around us. When we go out and do our best with our head held high, we can positively affect the environment around us. When I talk about Leveling Up Your Life and success, it doesn't always have to be tied to a goal. It's a way of living. It's how you carry yourself. It's how you treat others. It's the good feeling that comes back to you when you do good for others. The world needs more of this. More people doing their best and giving it their all, rather than waiting for everyone else to do it. Doing your best and putting good out into the world will not only come back to you (something I truly believe in), but the world will be a better place.

I want to end with this. You never know who is watching you. Whether you go out and do your best or when you do the exact opposite, people are always watching you. This can go for all areas of life. For example, let's say you publicly shared a big goal on social media to build a new business, commit to a new weight loss journey, or tackle that home project you have been thinking about. You begin openly talking about and sharing your progress and your journey. Some people will cheer you on, like your post, or send you a private message about what you are doing. Tons of people will never say a word, like your post, or comment. But they are watching. They always are. They are watching to see if you will stick with it or if you are going to give up. They won't openly like your post or comment, but they are there. I call these people "window watchers." They never actually engage with what you are doing, but they watch from the window. Maybe they are even thinking of joining your business or jumping on board with your new healthy lifestyle.

But then life happens. Life gets hard. You slowly post less and less about your new venture, and, eventually, you stop entirely. You don't talk about it as much, or maybe

> **LEVELING UP YOUR LIFE — IS A WAY OF LIVING, HOW YOU CARRY YOURSELF, AND HOW YOU TREAT OTHERS.**

don't talk about it at all. Now here is the point I am trying to make. You didn't know it at the time, but a few people were very interested in what you were doing. They were going to message you or reach out to join you possibly. But guess what? They are now gone, and you didn't even know they were interested. Why? Because you gave up, and they walked away. You didn't give your best, and that "window watcher" is now gone. This applies to all areas of your life. People are always watching you and what you do or don't do. People saw what you said you would do and then they watched you stop. Don't worry about what others think of you, but rather understand that any opportunities on your horizon could be gone instantly because you decided to settle, give up, and be average. Nothing good comes from just doing the bare minimum or putting forth anything other than our best effort. Yes, we will all have bad days, but that's not an excuse to be average in any given situation. You will guarantee one thing. You'll fail with that goal. Plus, you missed a potentially more significant opportunity on a bigger scale because you stopped.

Don't live your best life to appease others, but live your best life so that you seize all the opportunities that come your way and live up to the potential God has in store. Please do it for yourself and others that surround you every day, especially those most important to you, like your family. I do it for them, and I challenge you to do the same.

CHAPTER 14

EVERYTHING HAPPENS FOR A REASON

"Fuel your faith. Starve your fears."

John C. Maxwell

This is one of the most challenging life philosophies to understand because it makes sense only *after* something happens. Rarely do we reach our goal within the timeframe we thought we could achieve it. Simply writing this book has taken me longer than I ever anticipated. Understanding that everything happens for a reason and having faith in God that the current journey or struggle you are undertaking is all part of the process of life. I truly believe that the challenges we face are there for a reason – to make us stronger and be prepared for what else may come. If we are never challenged, we will never grow.

> **IF WE ARE NEVER CHALLENGED, WE WILL NEVER GROW.**

My parents divorced when I was in high school. This event impacted my life in many ways at the time. My father moved out after having an affair, so my mom raised my sister, brother, and me by herself, and during our adolescence. I went to a private Catholic school during my childhood and teenage years with hopes of going to a private Catholic college. However, that wasn't possible due to the financial burden that a private Catholic university would have created and my family situation with my parents.

I ended up attending the University of Albany. It wasn't my first choice but a State school was more affordable and realistic for my life. Pursuing my goal of playing baseball at the college level, the team tryout was one of the first things I signed up for.

I clearly remember tryouts and how well I performed. During high school, I was both a pitcher and outfielder on the team – and I was pretty good – so, I first tried out for pitcher of the Great Danes. I remember how hard I was throwing the ball. During tryouts I struck out one of the best players on the team at the time, which caught the coach's attention. The Coach came up to me after tryouts that day and told me how impressed the coaches were with me. They were looking forward to having me be part of the Great Danes.

Something I'll never forget happened next. The Head Coach told everyone the expectations for the team members. One of those requirements was attendance at *all* the practices, which were held during the afternoon. I had a major problem. I worked part time at Macy's to help pay for school. Due to my parents' recent divorce, financially, I had to work to get through school. I remember calling my dad, telling him what the Coach had said, and asking for some more money so I could play baseball. He listened to me and then said he was sorry, but he couldn't help. I stood there as still as a statue.

I was near the first baseline staring into the distance at the fence along the foul line. It wasn't the answer I was hoping for. I felt an immediate pit at the bottom of my stomach. I hung up the phone, walked over to the Head Coach, and told him my dilemma. I was hoping he would say don't worry about it, but I knew deep down he just set some serious expectations. That week I got cut and never made the team. I e-mailed the Coach to find out what happened, but I already knew why. I got a generic e-mail back that it was in the team's best interest. My baseball dream of playing in the pros was over. My baseball career was over. It was a harsh reality I had to face at eighteen.

I share this with you because I learned about taking ownership of my life when I was in my college years. I learned about responsibility. As much as I wanted to play baseball, working at Macy's taught me about ownership and responsibility. I knew that if I wanted to get a college degree at that time, it was on me to make that happen.

University of Albany wasn't my first choice, as mentioned earlier. But I met my best friend Brink there, who made a massive impact on my life. If I had made the baseball team, I wouldn't have become as close to Brink as I did. My friends would have been my teammates.

I also became good friends with a co-worker at Macy's named Anthony. He also became very tight with Brink, and we were often together. Anthony and I are still buddies today. We don't get to hang out nearly as often, but when we catch up on a phone call or text, it's as if we were just together again.

If my parents' divorce hadn't happened, I might not have been at the University of Albany. Everything in my life for the better wouldn't have happened if I hadn't been at Albany. My parents' divorce was horrible to go through as a kid. At the time, I would ask, "Why? Why me?" Looking back today, I see why I went through it and why God put me on that path. To meet Brink. To meet Anthony. To work. To grow as a person to prepare me for other things in my life.

Everything happens for a reason, but while we are in the thick of it, we usually don't see it that way. So how do I deal with unexpected trials and tribulations today? I live by faith over fear. I fuel my faith, starve my fears, and learn to let go of control over what happens in my life. If I do my part, everything else is out of my control. It's then in God's hands, the universe's hands, or whatever you believe in. The point is that what you are going through right now or what you have been through was all supposed to happen to prepare you for what will come.

> I FUEL MY FAITH, STARVE MY FEARS, AND LEARN TO LET GO OF CONTROL OVER WHAT HAPPENS IN MY LIFE.

When I graduated from the State Police Academy, I was sent to Long Island to do field training, where you ride along with a veteran

Trooper for twelve weeks to gain hands-on experience. I lived on Long Island, so it was great to be home, but I also knew this wasn't my permanent assignment, and I could be sent anywhere in the State once my field training was over. I was ultimately assigned to the State Police Barracks in Peekskill, NY, which was about an hour and a half from home (as long as there was no traffic).

I didn't want to be transferred there, commute daily, permanently move away from my family, or start a new life. I soon discovered that commuting daily back and forth through New York City traffic wasn't sustainable. I had no choice. It was my job, and I had to do it. I rented a house with a few other State Troopers in the same position, away from home and hoping to get transferred back. A few months later, I met my wife, Kristen – and the rest is pretty much history. She was from the area. Her family lived there, and I soon knew going back home to Long Island wasn't happening.

I have been happily married to Kristen for almost nineteen years and have three beautiful daughters. If I hadn't been assigned to Peekskill, none of this would have happened. Kristen wouldn't be in my life, and I wouldn't have three amazing daughters. At the time, I wasn't thrilled about going, but everything happens for a reason, right? You bet it does. Faith over fear.

One of my biggest goals as a State Trooper was to be a member of the elite SWAT Team, aka the Mobile Response Team (MRT). As you know, I was an ocean lifeguard, ran the NYC Marathon twice, and was very into fitness, so I was naturally intrigued by the highly fit group of people performing on this team. It was exciting, it seemed fun, and how cool would it be to be part of the group that the Troopers call on for help when they need emergency assistance? I was all over this!

Our MRT wasn't your typical police SWAT Team. It trains with some of the country's very best military and SWAT teams, even at the federal level. Candidates attended a grueling, six-month long training academy where we slept in barracks. Making the MRT was highly challenging and selective, but I set my eyes on it and began training. I ran daily, did push-ups, sit-ups, bench press, pull-ups, and anything else to keep me extremely fit. I worked every single day for this team. Tryouts only came around every few years, and I remember the day my opportunity arrived.

The tryout started with push-ups, sit-ups, and then the run. Next there was a bench press, an obstacle course, and a swim, fully clothed while holding a rifle out of the water. The run, the push-ups, and the sit-ups were based on the Cooper Fitness Test Norms, a scale correlating your age with the number of sit-ups, for example, that you need to achieve to land in a certain percentile. My goal was to be the best in each of the three areas. I remember doing the push-ups first. My goal was one hundred push-ups to max out the Cooper Norm score. The MRT Sergeant counting my push-ups was a former Army Ranger. More than half the time, he wouldn't count them. He just kept saying, "Didn't count. Didn't count. Didn't count." I was highly frustrated. He didn't say exactly what I was doing that was wrong. I kept going and still hit my goal of one hundred push-ups, but I did more like 175. I was exhausted.

I was in a group of ten people. We were split up into groups of three, but I was the odd man out, so I did the push-ups last. As soon as I was finished, the same Sergeant who discounted so many of my push-ups told me to start the sit-up test. I got no break. Guess what happened next? He did the same thing with my sit-ups. As soon as I started, he started in with, "Didn't count. Didn't count. Didn't count." Say what? As soon as the sit-up timed limit was up, he said, "You didn't meet the minimum. You are done." Just like that, I was disqualified from the tryouts. I didn't even get to do the other parts of the test. It was over. I had to sign the exit form that I was leaving and head back to the barracks I was assigned.

I heard this Sergeant was very biased against Troopers who hadn't been in the military. I also know a lot of the guys I was trying out with were in the military, so maybe he was striving to get them? I feel that to this day, he had it out for me. I wasn't in the military; therefore, he wasn't going to let me finish. He also had other MRT Troopers counting the push-up and sit-up repetitions, except for me. He was the one that counted for me. Very odd. Or was it? I'll explain why shortly. Also, I was told that no one else had over 50 percent of their push-ups and sit-ups not counted except for me.

A few years later, I was promoted to Investigator, just as MRT tryouts came around again. Many of the MRT members at the time wanted me to try out again. I had become friends with many of them before the tryouts, and they told me to give it another shot. The problem was that I wasn't eligible as an Investigator, only Troopers were. I put in a request to my Superintendent's Office to be able to try out for the MRT. If I made it, I would be open to taking the reduction in rank back to Trooper. I was ultimately denied, and I never got to try out. This was also the same time Brink tried out, and he subsequently made it.

This is what I learned looking back. When I was disqualified, I remember walking across the field with some tears in my eyes. No shame in sharing this. It was all I wanted to do at the time, and it was gut-wrenching to be singled out and forced into failure. Then, when I was denied to try out a second time, it became even more disheartening. About a year after the second tryout, Brink was killed on the MRT. If I had made that team, there was a chance I would have been in the same shootout as Brink and not be here today. The business I built wouldn't have happened. I wouldn't be a keynote motivational speaker, and I wouldn't be writing this book. Everything happens for a reason and, in a way, maybe I owe a thank you to that Sergeant that had it out for me. Indirectly perhaps he saved my life.

> **WORK WITH WHAT YOU HAVE AND WHERE YOU ARE BECAUSE WHAT YOU HAVE IS PLENTY.**

You may be at a point in your life that makes no sense. You may be questioning the career path you chose. You may question all the problems you are having. You may even have a deep-rooted fear or hate because of something you are going through. But remember, it is happening for a reason. It always does. So, how do you move forward?

I like to say work with what you have and where you are because what you have is plenty. Don't focus on something that seems so far away. Focus on what's in front of you and know it's enough to take you to the next level. Give your very best each day and know it's the right path even if you don't understand it. It wasn't easy, but looking back on my life, everything I went through led to something bigger and more significant.

Diamonds in their original form are pieces of coal. They need to be heated to extreme temperatures, put under intense pressure, and then cut and polished to become the diamonds we appreciate. You may not like the path your life is taking right now, but the daily stress and challenges you face are creating a new you. You need to experience the tough times to get to that next level, and, more times than not, it doesn't happen on your timeline. Have faith. Starve those fears and understand it's all happening for a reason. One day you will look back and know exactly why.

I BELIEVE IN YOU

Living the Leveled Up Life is not meant to be easy, nor is it meant for you to only excel in one area of your life. Instead, be aware that how you show up in all areas of your life is truly important. All you do in life, how you show up, handle tribulations, and take action each day must be in synergy with all the principles in *The Leveled Up Life*. This will develop a strong character and mindset that will propel your professional and personal life to another level. But remember, you can't just act this way on the days you feel like it. It has to become a way of life. It has to become a way of living. It has to become so engrained in your DNA that no one will ever question it.

It doesn't happen overnight, nor should it. Be patient. It may take years to master and develop the Leveled Up Life principles in all areas of your life. Understand that you must always be a student. You must always be learning. Even if you feel you have mastered *The Leveled Up Life*, continue to read other books. Continue to listen and study other successful people because success leaves clues.

Always be willing to learn because we always have room for improvement. Be obsessed each day with improvement. In the end, I truly believe that if the world read this book, it would be a better place. Not only would people be much more successful in their life largely, but there would be less hate, less anger, less stress, less frustration, and more happiness, joy, and positive energy in this world. Share it with a friend.

Now it's time you go out there and live your Leveled Up Life. Not just because you deserve to live up to your potential, but because those closest to you, those you love deserve the best version of you. They don't deserve the 50-percent you. They don't deserve the halfway you. They deserve the person who was meant to live up to their potential.

People will never remember all the materialistic things you own, such as a car or home, but people will never forget how you made them feel and the impact you created. It's time you live *your* Leveled Up Life. It's your turn. It's been your turn. Now take ownership and live your best life.

avid Atkins is a retired New York State Police Captain after twenty-two years of service. He ran all State Police operations for the entire County of Westchester, NY, which averages approximately four- to five-hundred thousand 911 calls a year throughout the entire county. David was the New York State Trooper of the Year in 2003 followed by New York State Police Investigator of the Year in 2007.

He moved up through the ranks during his twenty-two-year career with the New York State Police. He went from patrol to Investigations to leading undercover units involved in Organized Crime, Auto Theft, Money Laundering and large-scale drug organizations. David was also a first responder at Ground Zero on 09/11, where he spent weeks working in New York City.

Additionally while working full time with the NY State Police, David also built a million-dollar direct sales business.

Through his success both in law enforcement and business David became a Keynote Motivational Speaker presenting to groups of a few hundred people to over twenty thousand people in the NFL Superdome in New Orleans. Most importantly David is a husband and a father to his three daughters.

Made in the USA
Middletown, DE
16 August 2023

36785403R00099